Wood You Believe

VOLUME 6

THE SPIRITUAL SELF

A SPIRITUALITY OF HEALING
AND INTEGRATION
FOR THE TIMES WE LIVE IN

Fr Jim Cogley

Foreword by Brian D'Arcy

ISBN-10: 1642542555
ISBN-13: 978-1642542554

Any people depicted in stock imagery provided by Thinkstock are models,
and such images are being used for illustrative purposes only.
Certain stock imagery © Thinkstock.

This book is printed on acid-free paper.

Because of the dynamic nature of the Internet, any web addresses or links contained in this book may have changed
since publication and may no longer be valid. The views expressed in this work are solely those of the author and do not
necessarily reflect the views of the publisher, and the publisher hereby disclaims any responsibility for them.

Fr. Jim Cogley's Other Books in Matchstick Literary

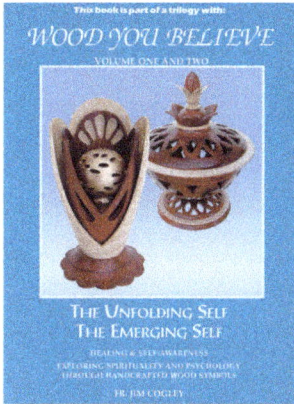

Wood You Believe Volume 1 & 2
The Unfolding Self
The Emerging Self

SEE WOOD IN A NEW LIGHT
SEE YOURSELF IN THE LIGHT OF WOOD.

Allow you de per Self to unfold as you enjoy a fascinating journey of self-discovery and spiritual awareness with symbols and wisdom that speak to your soul.

Recognize your Worth	*Reappraise your Past*
Realize your Potential	*Revive your Relationships*
Reclaim your Identity	*Resume after Loss*
Restore your Confidence	*Recover from Depression*
Reunite with your Inner Child	*Review your Priorities*
Resolve your Conflicts	*Reawaken your Humour*
Revisit old Memories	*Release your Creativity*
Reconsider your Anger	*Rediscover your True Self*

These are just some of the topics covered in Volume One and Two of Wood You Believe, where Fr.Jim Cogley, with twenty-five years experience of working in this area, combines the wisdom of spirituality and psychology, with the discipline of woodturning, to provide a multitude of fascinating symbols and life changing insights.

Readers' comments:

Filled with wisdom and insight this book is a masterpiece. It is well written, visually stunning and a feast for the soul.

From reading Wood You Believe I have learned to befriend the broken and fragmented parts of myself.

As someone who never read about psychology or spirituality before this book has transformed my life.

Reading Wood You Believe was a healing experience in itself.

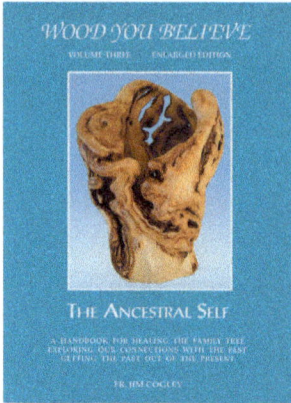

Wood You Believe Volume 3
The Ancestral Self

**SEE WOOD IN A NEW LIGHT
SEE YOURSELF IN THE LIGHT OF WOOD
UNDERSTAND WHO YOU ARE
IN THE LIGHT OF YOUR FAMILY TREE**

Don't allow the past to determine
how your life should be in the future.
Free yourself from old scripts.
Bring healing to your family Tree.

Remember your Ancestors	*Resolve old Conflicts*
Recognize old Patterns	*Reflect on Abortion*
Release old Hurts	*Revisit Memories and Places*
Recover from Illness	*Reawaken Ancestral Gifts*
Reclaim your Identity	*Reconnect with Providence*
Rededicate old Places	*Redeem your Family Tree*
Restore what was Lost	*Revive your Relationships*
Reunite with Lost Siblings	*Recover from Family Trauma*

These are just some of the topics covered in Wood You Believe - The Ancestral Self, wheere Fr. Jim Cogley, with twenty-five years experience of working in this area, combines the wisdom of spirituality and psychology, with the discipline of woodturning, to provide a multitude of fascinating symbols, life changing insights and some valuable resources of healing.

Readers comments:

The Ancestral Self adds an exciting new dimension to tracing your family tree.

For years I have been reading self-help books and searching for answers. Now I am finally asking the right questions.

The Ancestral Self is the book that many are waiting for. It contains so many keys for making sense of our lives.

I never realized that a lifelong burden was older than myself and could be lifted.

This is one book that delivers much more than it promises.

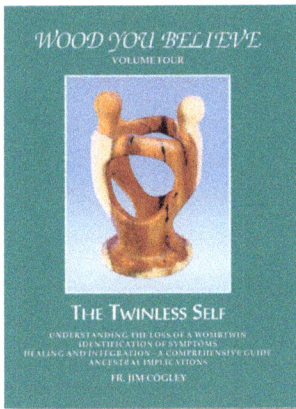

Wood You Believe Volume 4
The Twinless Self

What we don't know can still deeply affect us!

This book contains groundbreaking material that expands the horizons of self-awareness. For many people it has implications that are enormous and far reaching.

It is a medical fact that more than one in eight people began their journey into life not on their own. They had a wombtwin or were part of a multiple pregnancy.

It is a medical fact that for every set of twins born, at least on in five were triplets.

There is ever increasing evidence that the memory of this early loss can be carried through life as a form of psychological trauma that has previously been unrecognized and usually misdiagnosed. The symptoms of having experienced loss in the womb, or shortly after, include:

A sadness and sense of loss that persists
A loneliness that eats into the bones
A difficulty with close relationships
A burden of guilt that is irrational
A black hole that nothing can fill
A tendency towards isolation
A creativity that is stunted
A difficulty with letting go
A search that is endless
A depressive mentality
A restlesness of spirit
A poor sense of self

Whether the twin loss took place during the first few months, in the latter stages of the pregnancy, during or after birth, the symptoms seem to vary very little.

Could this be you or someone that you know? If so this book could shed light on the mysterious world of what its like to be a wombtwin survivor and point the way towards healing and recovery. Here are the stories of so many who discovered the key to the mystery that had plagued them all their lives. Written in language that is easily understood, the steps towards identification and resolution are clearly outlined.

Here is a book that could truly change your life
It could be the most important book you will ever read

FOREWORD BY FR BRIAN D'ARCY

For me the entire Wood You Believe series is insightful, helpful and challenging. Reading through Volume 6 I found myself highlighting and under-lining gems in every paragraph. This latest volume is an extremely important contribution to those of us struggling to find a healthy way through the present crisis in our beloved church. Healing and integration were never more needed in both society and church.

Father Jim explains what the basic problems are with clarity and honesty. Furthermore, from his experience in spirituality, art and psychotherapy, he provides a holistic and achievable process which might help bring about healing in the midst of the crisis which is tearing at the heart out of so many reflective people today. His insight that there are four common responses to a crisis – ignore, deplore, restore and explore – gave me a sense of solidarity and trust.

This is a book we are invited to reflect on and not just read. There are some serious issues dealt with – none more contentious than that of the sexual abuse of children. What the author proposes needs to be reflected upon deeply.

In an age when so many feel they have to leave their religion to find God, this superb work is at once accessible and profound. It challenges us to deal with the past respectfully so that we may discover our faith journey in the contemporary world. Typically there are beautiful pictures of his woodcraft which illustrate his writing and raise our thoughts to the sublime – as only good art can.

I recommend Volume 6 wholeheartedly for its loving critique of our church by one who cares deeply and who continues to give his life generously to so many fellow pilgrims.

Fr Brian D'Arcy, C.P.
Journalist and broadcaster

Praise for A Spirituality of Healing and Integration

To create from nothing - creatio ex nihilo - is to describe the work of the Father; it is to marvel at all that is, to value the gift of Life and all the beauty about us.

This book looks at the gifts of the co-worker, the creator from something, the fashioner, the turner of the wood who sees possibilities, who brings forth something new and powerful, something symbolic which offers meaning, without words.

Fr. Jim's creative talent is exceptional. Besides the beauty of the carvings, there is communication through symbol, that speaks from and to the deeper self, to discover the hidden, to give expression and voice to that which lies beneath and which is called forth.

The dynamic between artist and art, between symbol and meaning, between reflection and hope continues in this new volume.

+Denis Brennan.
Bishop of Ferns

A Spirituality of Healing and Integration offers much needed wisdom for the spiritual landscape we find ourselves in at this time. The inspiring symbolism, intertwined with scripture, story and insights from psychology, makes it a compelling read. It outlines succinctly and clearly where we have come from and where we find ourselves as Church in Ireland today. But it doesn't stop there: it navigates us towards a spirituality of the future and offers a direction in which we can orientate ourselves in religious practice. Fr Jim has much to say about the requirement for holistic spiritual formation which needs to integrate both psychological and spiritual growth. Through sharing his concepts of ancestral healing, integration of the shadow, reclaiming the True Self, etc., we are led to a view of a transformative Christian Spirituality. Fr Jim has his finger on the pulse when, for example, he says that, 'Neither a spirituality that ignores the dynamics of psychological growth nor a psychology that denies the spiritual nature of the person can serve as an adequate guide for people today.' The B-Attitudes outlined near the end of the book sum up much of the vision offered in Vol 6 … Blessed are those who live life with open hands, for they are ready to receive.

Martina Lehane Sheehan,
Psychotherapist, spiritual director and author

… Of his work so far, this is Jim Cogley's most enterprising achievement, as it testifies in word and wood symbol to his belief that an interweave of psychology and spirituality have an integrating function for the soul and indeed for the whole person. Never before, given the current state of the Irish Church, were Cogley's multi-skilled talents more sorely needed. Like Kavanagh he believes that faith is worthless unless it is energising, young and elemental.

Sr Una Agnew SSL,
Author

This book is a real gem. It is profound and seductively readable. It makes the perfect gift and I would love if every Catholic in Ireland had the opportunity to read it. To be aware of the impact of the last 150 years on our lives is very necessary to move towards self-understanding and acceptance. Only then can we begin the journey towards healing, integration and transformation.

Fr Seamus Whitney, Kiltegan Missionaries,
Director of Slí an Chroí Retreat Centre

Volume 6 is a beautiful, enlightening book acknowledging the human questioning and struggle involved in a search for new meaning and hope. The use of symbols, psychology and theology creates a powerful guide to enter our hearts, embrace the True Self and re-emerge with a new sense of the Divine within.

Josephine Murphy,
Co-Founder of Personal Counselling Institute

This is a deceptively simple little book that is quite profound. It is laced with intriguing wisdom, insights and stories. The language is contemporary and expresses in a very succinct manner what the Christian Way is all about.

It will be of particular benefit for those who have given up on their faith practice yet still want to explore their Christian heritage and seek what they may have been missing.

Gerry and Mary Carberry,
Resurrexit Community

TABLE OF CONTENTS

Part 3 – A Faith Experienced

Introduction

In May 2012, I was invited to give a keynote address to the former students of PCI (Personal Counselling Institute) at their annual gathering in the Emmaus Retreat Centre, Swords, Co. Dublin. This was also a memorial day in honour of a founder member, Liam McCarthy. Nearly a hundred psychotherapists took part in the event and the talk entitled *The Integration of Spirituality and Psychology* was well received. Several suggested that it should be published in order to reach a wider audience. All of the material from that presentation is included in this Volume 6 and it has also been expanded upon and extended considerably.

Of the six volumes in the popular *Wood You Believe* series, this is the one I believe to be by far the most important and without doubt the most challenging. Its aim is to capture as accurately as possible where we find ourselves in relation to our present religious crisis. In Part One and Two it outlines where we have come from on our Catholic journey over the past 150 years, how that legacy impacts upon us today, and where we might presently be in our faith experience. For some of the background material I am indebted to Sr Una Agnew and her work, *The Mystical Imagination of Patrick Kavanagh.*

While acknowledging that we are products of our history, this book invites us not to reject it but rather to critically review our past so that we do not become its prisoners. For anyone struggling to make sense of our current faith crisis and what is happening today this little book might be a real gift – even manna from Heaven.

The third and larger part of this work focuses on the core elements of Christ's teaching and the essential aspects of discipleship that have often been hidden in plain sight or buried altogether beneath so many layers of historical accretions. It explores the journey towards the True Self as our spiritual quest and ultimately, our journey to God. Along the way, it embraces the centrality of Christ, the role of suffering and the place of the Cross.

Wood You Believe is the overall title of the series and is particularly appropriate for this work since it integrates psychology and spirituality; the *You* of the personal journey and *Believe* of the faith dimension, through the medium of *Wood*. Handcrafted symbols are interspersed throughout, providing a visual representation of the truths expressed.

PART 1

A FAITH QUESTIONED

THE TRUTH THAT PREVAILS

On the cover of this book and depicted below is an unusual piece of artwork. It is a rather rough-looking piece of bog oak, more than four thousand years old that almost completely overshadows a small Celtic cross. Initially, our attention may be drawn to the bog oak but slowly it moves to the cross underneath. It's a symbolic piece that can represent the truth that the Christian faith and its message still remain as intact, as relevant and as vibrant as ever, in spite of being overshadowed for centuries by so many dark forces and layers of historical accretions.

A Faith Overshadowed

I would like to name some of those layers and share a few reflections in relation to faith and spiritual maturity – where we have come from historically, where we might find ourselves at present and how we can move forward, particularly within the Irish context. Also, to uncover some of the core truths that makes Christianity unique among the great world religions. As a priest and psychotherapist with over thirty years' experience, I have had the opportunity and privilege to reflect deeply on these matters and in this publication, I take the opportunity to share the 'distilled essence' of my thoughts.

FROM RELIGIOUS PRACTICE TO FAITH EXPERIENCE

The vast majority of people who walk this planet hold the opinion that there is a God. An ever-decreasing number try to deny his or her existence. Many of these belong to the 'Thank-god-I'm-an-atheist brigade, so my life is my own and I can do with it as I please.' Then there are the vast numbers of believers who are faithful to their religious beliefs and practices. Yet another group fall into the category of faithfully practicing but who are crippled by doubts and feel they are only paying lip service to their beliefs without their hearts being in it. Finally, there are those for whom God is an experience so real that they don't have to believe: they just know. These are the ones who have moved from religious practice to religious experience. The Swiss psychiatrist, Carl Jung, was asked towards the end of his life if he believed in God? He replied, 'I don't have to believe any longer. I just know. I just know that I know.'

It is now obvious to everyone that the Catholic Church as an institution is going through one of the greatest crises in its history. Catholicism stands at a threshold where enduring questions are crying out for imaginative and gospel-based responses. Many would agree with the late Cardinal Montini when he said that it is two hundred years behind the times. I refer here to Church as institution because most people can make a distinction between the Church as the local community and the Church as a hierarchical institution. Yet, it is also true that there is a considerable degree of bewilderment and confusion at present, especially for those who have grown up with and have had their faith in that old institutional model. They now feel betrayed by the Church they were once so faithful to and do not know where to turn to for guidance and answers.

THE FAITH CRISIS OF OUR TIME

In the face of a crisis there are four common responses:

The first is to **IGNORE**. This is the ostrich approach: to bury our heads in the sand and hope that the storm will eventually blow over and to not get blown over with it. There are many traditionalist Church personnel and laity who fall into this category, with the attitude that 'the Church has survived for two thousand years and will be there for a long while yet, so let's not get too worried. There's no need to rock the boat; we just keep doing what we have always done and all will be well'. The Church may well survive but undoubtedly the writing is on the wall that it will not survive, as we have known it. We are in a time of transition when the old is dying and the new is slowly coming to birth: a time when we either choose change or have change forced upon us. How we see ourselves and our role at present is crucial, whether as hospice workers with the old or as midwives to the new. We may need to choose whether we want to be associated with that which is dying or with that which is being born: with death or life!

The second is to **DEPLORE**. This is to complain about the terrible state of affairs we find ourselves in, to pin blame on those we deem responsible, but not be any way proactive in bringing about change. It may take the form of giving out about the decline in religious practice and lack of interest while failing to ask the hard question regarding why it is in decline. Focusing in on questions like priestly celibacy and the ordination of women rather than our lack of an incarnational model of spirituality as the real issue is also characteristic of this simplistic view. Fixing the blame rather than fixing the problem is the hallmark of this approach.

The third is to **RESTORE**. This is to try and move forwards by going backwards. Return to the way things were without questioning if they ever worked in the first place. This is to become more traditionalist and ultra conservative, and to promote a right-wing agenda. The call to return to more traditionalist values usually ignores the practices that were condoned during a traditionalist era. These included the widespread use of corporal punishment as an essential tool in our shame-based educational system, the extent of institutional abuse and the inhumane treatment of unmarried mothers, to name but a few. The scandal of clerical sex abuse represents the greatest cover up of all and represents the demise of clericalism, as it has been known for hundreds of years.

Thinking Outside the Box

The fourth is to **EXPLORE**. This is to face the present crisis, ask the relevant questions, to see all sorts of wonderful possibilities arising from it and to move forward in a spirit of hope. It is to be creative and find new ways and a new language for expressing the age-old truths. An outmoded religious language is one of the greatest turn offs for a new generation. The age-old truths remain the same but the language we use to express them needs to continually change. Thinking outside the box that has become too small and constrictive is the key that unlocks the Divine potential. The end of an old system can be the rebirth of something new and exciting. An old model of Church as institution and an outmoded way of doing things can give way to a Vatican II vision of Church as The People of God on a pilgrim journey where all are equal but exercising different ministries.

OUR CURRENT SCHISM

At this time there is an undeclared and ever-widening schism between the two latter aforementioned camps: one wanting to move backwards and the other willing to go forward. Many Catholics are asking whether it is necessary to buy into a right-wing agenda or instead have the courage to forge ahead even though it may be a wintertime for progressives. Many feel that, sooner rather than later, they may have to make that choice not because they want to but because it is being forced upon them. In the ecclesiastical climate of recent decades there was little room for a loyal opposition or openness to debate on certain important issues. Neither was there any apparent appreciation for creative diversity which is an essential component of all true unity. While the Church does not need unloving criticism it does need to be open to critical love, especially from those who really care. As this book is being completed Pope Francis has just been elected bringing a new sense of hope that an ecclesiastical springtime is possible. His new style of leadership, and willingness to 'bend' the rules, could point to a new openness to creativity and diversity offering freedom from the stifling orthodoxy and regressive approach of recent times.

From listening to people sharing their faith at seminars and faith gatherings in so many places throughout Ireland and beyond, it is obvious that there is a profound spiritual awakening occurring at this time. It is interesting that it seems to be experienced most by those who are grappling with painful issues and deeply engaged on their human journey: those suffering addictions, and victims of abuse, separation and tragedy. Ironically, it is least evident within the mainstream churches and among the faithful remnant who are the good practicing believers. So it would seem paradoxical that many have had to lose their religion in order to find their God and experience spiritual awakening. It is not uncommon to meet someone who has not set foot in church for years and find that they have a profound spiritual connection. Yet, that same depth of spirit is not as easy to find in regular churchgoers who may have been faithful to a lifetime of religious practice.

THE FAITH JOURNEY

Why is the phenomenon of finding faith in the most unlikely places so common? A useful model for understanding the faith journey is to think of it in three stages. The first is 'unquestioning acceptance' where we believe everything that others around us believe. The second is 'questioning non-acceptance' where we might not believe anything we are told until we find it to be true for ourselves and the third is 'spiritual awakening' which is coming home to mature adult faith.

Where have the vast majority of practicing believers been stuck but in the first stage of 'unquestioning acceptance' with the result that it never became real for them. Any form of questioning was actively discouraged in our recent tradition and growing up I got the impression that to question my faith was to run the risk of losing it. So we tended to remain in the immature faith of childhood where we were given answers but denied the right to first ask the questions. Our society today is by and large highly educated in almost every area except the Christian faith. Religion, for the remnant who are practicing, has largely remained at the operational level of primary school and by and large even the rudiments of faith are not understood.

As a result of the recent scandals and the enforcement of a more sinister right-wing agenda, (where even freedom of speech has been suppressed) many traditional believers find themselves being pushed out of their comfort zones of unquestioning acceptance into the uncomfortable situation of having more questions than answers. There is widespread disillusionment with the Church as institution; a perception that it seems to be losing its way and a sense that the rug is being pulled from beneath our feet. This in itself can be very good because for many, religious practice may have been little more than a safety net that provided a false sense of security. Now in a state of confusion, and not knowing whether to look right or left, they are being forced to look within for what they really believe. This new journey may well be the first stage of genuine awakening. As Carl Jung said, 'The one who looks within awakens.'

Being able to live with questions is a real sign of growth to maturity while it is a feature of those who were most insecure in childhood to still feel the need to be bound by rules and regulations and to be spoon-fed with easy answers. A right-wing agenda feeds directly into this and has always been a feature of religious fundamentalism. The quote from the poet Maria Rilke is particularly appropriate: 'Be patient with all that is unsolved in your heart and try to love the questions themselves. Do not seek answers that cannot be given you. Live the questions now and one day you will live along some distant day into the answer.' The Islamic sage Al-Ghazali who said that, 'Knowledge is a box and there is no doubt that the question is the key', would be in total agreement.

UNLOCKING SPIRITUAL TRUTHS

Nut and Bolt Box

What appears to be an ordinary nut and bolt made of wood, when unscrewed, turns out to be a box containing a little angel. So many of our Christian beliefs – the nuts and bolts that hold together our religion – urgently need to be opened out in order to discover what they are really about and to find the beautiful life-giving truth they contain.

For myself, I seem to be involved in a lifelong process of sifting out the wheat from the chaff. There is such an amazing spiritual richness and profound psychological insights to be found in the Christian tradition but they have to be uncovered from the dross that has accumulated, particularly over the past 150 years. Tradition could be described as the living faith of the dead while traditionalism is the dead faith of the living. Our tradition is alive with wisdom while our traditionalism has become boring, irrelevant and out of touch with its roots, particularly its scriptural foundation. So many perform certain duties and take part in rituals but without any real sense as to why they are doing so except that it's what they have always done.

As a priest for over thirty years, I have enjoyed an uneasy relationship with the institutional Church. Yet I have always felt a strong call to work from within the system that has been the crucible of my formation. This has enabled me to criticise the organisation from within, using its own scriptures, saints and sources. During my college years, as I realised just how far the institution had become removed from the message, I was strongly tempted to shake the dust from my feet and take another path. However, following a whisper of Spirit that said, *Learn to be a leaven within rather than a smoking firebrand without*, I remained where I was. Looking back on the wisdom of that, I now deem it a privilege to have been able to unlock so many spiritual truths from the inside rather than to have spent over thirty years throwing stones from the outside, which I could so easily have done.

PART 2

A Faith Legacy

HOW DID WE ARRIVE WHERE WE ARE?

When I critically evaluate the brand of Catholicism that has been on offer in Ireland for the past 150 years I find myself reflecting first on the fear-based religion of my earlier years, with the constant focus on guilt and unworthiness, and the ever-present fear of some trivial misdemeanour being enough to put one in Hell for all eternity. This leaves me in almost total agreement with many of the sentiments expressed by Patrick Kavanagh. I would regard the Monaghan poet as being one of the most unlikely and yet best theological commentators on the religious state of affairs in Ireland since the Famine. It was from that period (from 1860 onwards) that Romanised Catholicism was strongly enforced. Up to this point, the vast majority of Irish people would not even have known which Pope occupied the chair of Peter. The individual responsible for the enforcement was Ireland's first cardinal, James Cullen, a man who had his roots in the Parish of Oylegate near Enniscorthy where I now find myself.

Many, like Kavanagh, felt Romanised Catholicism to be a betrayal of our Celtic tradition and spirituality. Unlike St Patrick, who had created a healthy precedent by incorporating the colours and mystical depths of paganism into his new teaching, Cardinal Cullen tried to eradicate the old by implanting the new. The result was that religion became less community orientated and more church-centred, hierarchical, over serious, and very legalistic. This was an era when all forms of questioning were supressed. You were told to keep the rules and the rules kept you. It was the time when, as Kavanagh said, people forgot how to smile in church, began to wear long faces and thought that the more they suffered the higher the place they were going to get in the next world. (*Kavanagh's Weekly*)

LIFELESS RELIGION

This Romanisation represented a turning point when Ireland was being forced to lose touch with its past, especially its Celtic spiritual tradition. It was a time when religion became guilt-ridden and legalistic having been greatly influenced by a heresy imported from France known as Jansenism. In his column, *Kavanagh's Weekly*, Kavanagh wrote, 'Somewhere in the nineteenth century … an anti-life heresy entered religion.' Jansenism had a deeply pessimistic view of human nature along with a belief in the virtual impossibility of being saved by God's grace. Salvation came more from rigorous adherence to rules and regulations than by God's favour. Jansenism was quite insidious in that it sapped the vitality of the people. It was an anti-life heresy that propounded a gloomy doctrine that our natural appetites were always in opposition to the God who gave them to us in the first place and where morality was seen, not as a protection for our soul, but as a boulder set to crush life. This was a time when we became obsessed with sexual sin and even dancing was regarded as an impediment to real holiness. It was not uncommon for priests to be seen on roads after dances armed with blackthorn sticks chasing couples away from 'dangerous occasions of sin.' Company keeping was denounced from the pulpits and theatre going was not allowed for priests. In seminaries, even newspapers were strictly forbidden. Religion had become serious business and the God of Fear had completely overshadowed the God of Love. (*Enthusiasm* by Ronald A. Knox)

An indication of how far removed from the truth we had drifted was easy to be seen in the way that the breach of man-made rules like eating meat on Friday, breaking a fast before going to Communion or missing Mass on Sunday were regarded as mortal sins and so equated with moral evil. A story is told of two men who met in Hell and the discussion arose as to how they ended up there. One said that he had committed murder. To which the other replied, 'You're lucky, because I'm here for something that isn't even a sin anymore!' In the words of a friend of mine to his twenty-something-year-old daughters, 'My ancestors are roasting in Hell for the kind of behaviour you take for granted.'

A criticism often levelled against the institutional Church is that it has been more into the love of power than the power of love. It was certainly regarded as authoritarian but authority properly understood means to empower. It comes from the Latin word *augere* which means, 'to make things grow'. So the question arises: has our experience been more of control than genuine authority?

This was a Church Kavanagh believed had failed miserably to respond to the needs of the people. He strongly advocated priests to return to real Catholicism and to root their religion in the sacredness of life. He also recommended that they learn to accept sin as commonplace and to look at it clearly and without fear. (*Kavanagh Weekly*)

The Catholicism of the time, he believed, lacked depth and was too sentimental and pious to have real roots. He concluded that what the Church needed was a new depth of spirituality and real backbone. The introduction of the new Roman-style religion had driven a wedge between life and spirituality whereas before, in the Celtic tradition, they were never separate. So he didn't mince his words when he said, 'This new religion was an almost complete negation of the Incarnation.' (*The Mystical Imagination of Patrick Kavanagh* by Una Agnew)

His 'new religion' is now our 'old religion' and in the words of the Prophet Ezekiel, 18:2, 'Because our fathers and mothers have been forced to eat sour grapes the children's teeth are set on edge.' We are those children, still open to the discovery of our spiritual nature but very wary of any beliefs or practices that do not enrich our lives. Unfortunately, many have thrown out the baby with the bathwater and by rejecting what was on offer their spiritual nature has become completely neglected. Thus, the next generation to come along are lacking a spiritual inheritance. The danger is that when we no longer believe in something we can so easily end up believing in anything. So the door is left wide open for the more nebulous spirituality often found in New Age literature and even for involvement in the sinister world of cults.

Deep at the core of that old-style religion was a distrust of our basic humanity and so all that was human – our desires, our emotions, our sexuality – had to be repressed, denied and beaten into submission. The only way that both Church and society knew how to control our baser instincts was through suppression. Yet, as we now know only too well, any aspect of ourselves and our human nature that we are not in a right relationship with will always come back, not necessarily to bite us, but to seek integration. So is it any wonder that the scandal of clerical sex abuse has come back to haunt the very institution that denounced sex so vehemently and which now heralds the very end of clericalism itself.

This denigration of our human reality promoted an image of holiness that the vast majority found completely unattainable. It was an image of rigid self-mortification that was deemed to suit only rare and gifted individuals. Perfection was understood as moral impeccability and religion was a worthiness contest of gaining brownie points. A saint was someone who had successfully avoided sin and not someone who had transcended sin. These so-called saints were the ones who were often so hard to live with precisely because what they had succeeded in doing was closing off the wellspring of their own humanity.

From the Jewish Talmud comes a story that encapsulates a common view of what so many used to think qualified one to be holy:

> A student of the Torah came to his teacher and announced that in his opinion he was qualified to become a rabbi. When asked what his qualifications were he replied, 'I have disciplined my body so that I can sleep on the ground, I can eat the grass of the field and allow myself to be whipped three times a day.'

> 'See that yonder white ass,' said the teacher, 'and be mindful that it sleeps on the ground, eats the grass of the field and is whipped no less than three times daily. Up to the present you may qualify to be an ass but certainly not a rabbi!'

BEFRIENDING OUR SHADOW

For so long there has been an almost complete denial of the shadow side of human nature. Coupled with teaching that encouraged the pursuit of perfection, there was the perfect mix to convey the impression that the pursuit of holiness and becoming fully human and fully alive were two entirely different paths. Perfection by its nature has to deny everything that is less than perfect. The problem then is that it becomes projected elsewhere and we can become judgmental and intolerant of others faults and failings. How we fall prey to projection so easily and see the splinter in someone else's eye while failing to recognise the plank in our own finds humorous expression in the following story:

A newly married woman at the breakfast table every morning passed remarks to her husband as to the dreadful state of her neighbour's washing; how she should be ashamed of putting out clothes on the line that were still so dirty and stained. One morning, she came down for breakfast and was surprised to see a line full of whiter-than-white clothes. She remarked to her husband that at long last her neighbour was doing it as it should be done and must have changed the washing powder. 'I don't think so;' the husband replied, 'you see I was up early this morning and I cleaned our windows.'

WHOLENESS

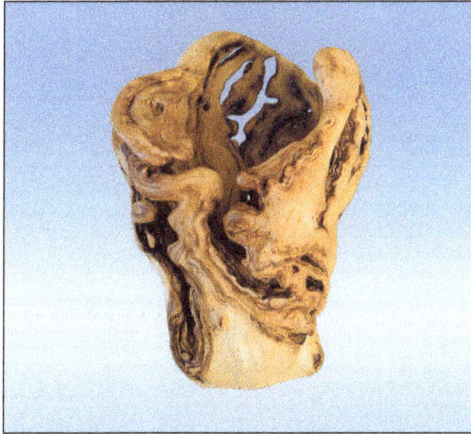

Perfectly Imperfect – Yet Perfectly Whole

The piece shown is from Vilnius in Lithuania. In all its contortions and distortions it seems to carry within itself the troubled history of its country of origin. It has been gutted and yet has emerged perfectly imperfect and still perfectly whole.

While our focus in the past has been on the impossible ideal of moral perfection, a much more useful model to work with is 'wholeness'. Like the piece of wood that can be both perfectly imperfect and yet perfectly whole, wholeness can incorporate all measures of imperfection. Such a model encourages us to take responsibility for our shadow side and offers the reassurance that it too can be transformed and have its place. In the words of Carl Jung, 'The shadow is pure gold,' provided it is accepted and allowed to form part of the picture of who we are – like the darkness and light expressed in the age-old symbol of the Yin-Yang.

SPIRITUAL FORMATION AND PSYCHOLOGICAL GROWTH

Yin -Yang

Back in the early '70s, I entered St Patrick's College Maynooth – the National Seminary. At that time, spiritual direction and psychology were perceived as going in opposite directions. If you needed counselling it was because you were deemed a failure in your spiritual life. As ridiculous as it seems, the personal story and the ancestral story did not have any place in the formation process. There was never a time or opportunity afforded for anyone to talk about their own personal journey. In fact any admission of weakness or having problems could be deemed as making you unfit for ordination. A door was effectively closed on your past as if it had never existed and there was no understanding of the way that earlier issues continue to influence our present reality. This was brought home to me recently when I met a fellow student whose room was adjacent to mine for two years. When he spoke about his own tragic childhood when both his parents had died, I was shocked to find myself hearing it for the first time. It took me some time to realise that the truly authentic spiritual path is the human journey and that the truly human and most fully alive human being is the one who gives most glory to God.

I would also say that it has taken – and is still taking – the world of psychology a long time to realise that without a spiritual dimension it too is a bird with only one wing and unable to fly. The human being is innately spiritual and without a sense of meaning, purpose and destiny cannot achieve his or her full potential.

Neither a spirituality that ignores the dynamics of psychological growth nor a psychology that denies the spiritual nature of the human person can serve as an adequate guide for people today who seek to live in greater harmony and integration.

God does not save us from our humanity but rather through our humanity.

Aboriginal Boomerang

Let us consider the boomerang as an analogy: the area where we have traditionally placed God is at the top while placing ourselves at the lower end with all of our broken and flawed humanity. The implication was that as long as we were in the state of grace we were on the upward road and going to Heaven and that it didn't matter if our human reality was in tatters and our life experience was abject misery. We were taught that suffering was good for our soul and we were advised to offer it up. It was as if we could close the door on all that was human and still become a spiritual person. Placing spiritual bandages over deep emotional wounds was the norm with the result that people often came to the end of their journey with a lifetime of emotional baggage that had never been transformed. As we now know that which we do not transform we transfer and so this unfinished business became the legacy for the next generation who were forced to carry what another had tried to disown.

GENERATIONAL HEALING

The movement of spirituality is always towards truth; the fullness of truth expressed in Jesus Christ. To those who believed in him, Jesus said, 'You will know the truth and the truth will set you free.' John 8:32. The work of psychotherapy is to uncover important aspects of that truth without which we cannot become whole. It is to facilitate the coming into awareness those parts of our personal and ancestral story that buried in the unconscious continue to control and influence out lives. If spirituality is about bringing that which was in darkness into the light then psychotherapy, sharing a similar goal, is its handmaid.

Family Tree Bowl

The carved bowl depicts a tree with its roots reaching down deep into the soil. In trees there is a condition known as 'root rot' which eventually travels up through the branches and extends to the leaves. Getting to the root cause of a problem is essential for healing to take place. Hebrews 12:15, contains a warning of not allowing a root of bitterness to take hold which can eventually poison the entire tree. It is self-evident from working with individuals in therapy that so often their problems are so much older than themselves and have roots stretching back into that person's family history. A major difficulty with forgiveness and a strong sense of injustice can be the legacy of a deep hurt that was never resolved in an earlier generation.

What one generation tries to forget another will be forced to remember. The most enduring legacy that parents leave to their children can never be written on paper. It is the unfinished business of their lives that live on in the next generation. The secrets that were safely guarded will sooner or later find expression in a burdened soul who may well end up with a mental breakdown. The mother who gave up her child for adoption and never spoke about it may fail to bond with her next child leaving that child with an acute sense of rejection. Or, she may live the life of the one she lost through another and be very possessive leaving him or her unfree and lacking a sense of identity.

Snails on the Run!

At first sight it might seem that the three snails with their shells on their backs should be led by the older and end with the younger. Where each represents a different generation the smaller goes first because the burden tends to increase rather than decrease with the passage of time. In so many families there is an enormous legacy of anger that has accumulated as each generation, failing to transform it, unconsciously transferred it to the next. For so long, children were given the message that anger was bad news and needed to be beaten into submission. Teaching our young people the importance of awakening their creativity through befriending their anger, rather than acting it out destructively, must surely be a priority. Our current crisis in society, of murders, stabbings, suicide and domestic violence, undoubtedly has a large generational component.

It has been estimated that ninety per cent of families are dysfunctional and the remaining ten per cent don't know that they are! Where a family is problematic, the answer is not to rush for the spiritual bandage of having a mass offered. This may be appropriate, but at the end, rather than the beginning, of a journey into truth. It is far more beneficial to first draw up a genogram and begin to look realistically at where the current problems are rooted: patterns that repeat with uncanny accuracy; old grievances that cry out for forgiveness; secrets that need to be broken; the voiceless that need a voice; grieving that was never completed; trauma that could never be faced; behaviour that needs to be understood. All of these and many more 'skeletons' need to be given flesh.

Past issues that remain unresolved are rarely to be found where people think they have been left – in the past – but are far more likely to be found in the here and now with what is happening in the lives of the current generation. It is a stark reality that so many families find themselves living in the broken remains of a past that is ever present. Without awareness, all our todays will be just yesterdays, as the past continues to blight the present.

FAMILY TREE BEATITUDES

Blessed are those who honour their ancestors,
For the gifts of those gone before shall be theirs.

Blessed are those who seek the truth,
For bringing freedom, it shall meet them halfway.

Blessed are those who are non-judgmental,
For they shall not be judged.

Blessed are those who remember,
For they shall not be forgotten.

Blessed are those who speak the unspoken,
For they are giving voice to the voiceless.

Blessed are those who own what is wrong,
For them the answer is close at hand.

Blessed are those who break the secret,
For because of their courage someone walks free.

Blessed are those who seek understanding,
For in them history shall not be repeated.

Blessed are those who seek where they come from,
For they shall find knowledge of who they are.

Blessed are those who forgive for an ancestor,
For through them the chains of bondage are broken.

Blessed are those who embrace the estranged,
For with them their place is forever assured.

Blessed are those who draw others to the Light,
For they shall be welcomed with eternal appreciation.

Jim Cogley

A more comprehensive treatment of Intergenerational Healing is to be found in Volume 3 – *The Ancestral Self.*

INCARNATION – A DOWNWARD PATH

Perhaps one of the most profound statements made in the last century was that of the Jesuit priest, Teilhard de Chardin, when he said that, 'We are not human beings trying to become spiritual. Instead we are spiritual beings having a human experience'. That being the case we are called to embrace all that it means to be human and in the process discover our spiritual nature. Such a statement seems utterly incarnational. If God becomes human and embraces all of our humanity then the journey for us is towards our humanity rather than away from it. In an incarnational model God is not at the top of the boomerang but closer to the bottom. In the words of Richard Rohr, 'God comes disguised as our life.' Having spent a lifetime believing that the goal of life was to get to Heaven could the real goal, based on an incarnational model, be to come to Earth – to become fully grounded in our humanity?

The piece entitled the Divine Embrace, reflects God's embrace of us in all of our humanness and also conveys the challenge to accept ourselves in all that it means to be human.

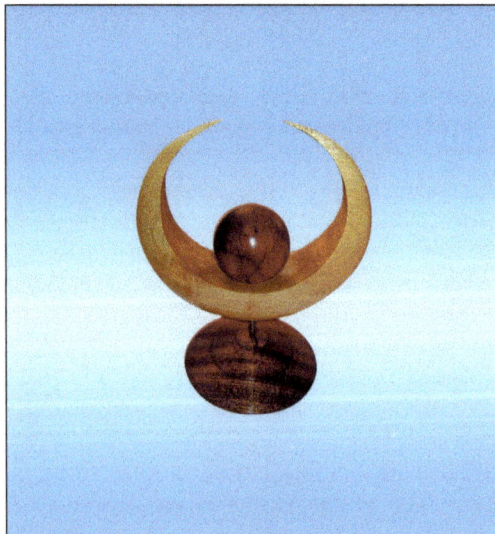

The Divine Embrace

In the Gospel of St Luke, Chapter 19, there is the story of the little man, Zacchaeus, who thought that in order to see Jesus he had to climb up a sycamore tree. Jesus, who is the Incarnation of Divinity, sees him up there and says, 'Zacchaeus, come down to my level, I want to dine with you.' In colloquial terms he could have said, 'Zacchaeus, you're barking up the wrong tree', and I wonder have we been doing the same? Perhaps the true Christian journey is not upwards after all but downwards or inwards into the discovery of the truly magnificent as well as the acceptance of the seemingly unacceptable side of ourselves.

Whether someone is trying to climb upward or prepared to journey inwards can be reflected in their attitude to the so-called modern day therapies that may not be modern at all. Examples might include Reflexology, Bio-energy, Aromatherapy and Chinese Medicine. These are often placed under the broad umbrella of 'New Age' by certain spiritual writers who usually warn their readers against engaging in such practices. However, all such therapies focus on, and help us to embrace, our human reality. So, if a writer is coming from a background that denies much of the human reality, is he or she not likely to demonise that which is foreign to them? While it is absolutely necessary to exercise discernment in relation to what is available it is also important to remember the saying of Jesus that, 'The wise scribe takes from his storehouse things both new and old'.

THE CALL FOR HEALING

Because our traditional religious practice was so inadequate in helping people face up to and deal with real life issues there remains an enormous legacy of hurt that deeply impinges on the faith life of so many believers and affects the quality of our liturgical celebrations. The practice of spiritualising unpleasant emotional events and 'offering them up' did not mean that they went 'up' but rather 'down' where they got buried in the recesses of the unconscious. This was akin to splitting off aspects of our human reality and in so doing being unaware of how they were going to affect our lives in the long term. It is entirely possible that the real scandals affecting the lives of people today are not the obvious ones in the public domain concerning how others were treated, but those less obvious internal ones of a personal nature that have never been addressed. Many common statements deserve to be taken not just at face value but interpreted in the light of unresolved issues that are crying out for attention. It is more often what is not being said that needs to be heard before a process of healing can begin.

- *I go to church but my heart is not in it.* This could be a statement of frustration that current Church structures and practices are too much at variance with gospel values and that there seems to be no willingness to listen to the signs of the times. At a deeper level it could be rooted in anger and indicate an emotional wound where the person feels out of touch with his or her heart. Particularly where issues of abuse and childhood trauma have not been resolved this becomes the experience of so many.

- *I don't attend church any longer.* The reasons for this are many and varied and could be just plain laziness and lack of attention to one's spiritual welfare. It may well be a reaction to the absence of meaningful liturgies at local level. Would we return to a restaurant where the food was served badly or where we went away hungry! It could also be a pointer to a time when that person no longer felt any connection between what was going on in their lives and what was being heard in church.

- *My faith and trust in God is not what it used to be.* Underlying this could be a serious disappointment or hurt where a dream was shattered and life didn't turn out as expected. Like Martha and Mary in John 11, when Jesus delayed in answering their plea to come and heal their brother and Lazarus lay in the tomb, both cried out, 'Lord, if only you had been here our brother would not have died.' Deep-seated emotional issues like unresolved grief can seriously affect our faith and ability to trust.

- *I am in the middle of a faith crisis and don't know what to believe.* On the surface this would appear to be a difficulty about believing in God. Probing deeper it is more likely to be about not being able to believe in oneself. It is a well-known fact that as a person's self-image improves so does their image of God. Failure to practice 'inner hospitality' towards the darker aspects of ourselves gives rise to self-criticism and fragmentation. Reconciliation with self is a necessary step for experiencing faith in God.

- *I am spiritual but not religious.* This usually indicates a solitary journey where childhood faith has been discarded and traditional practice does not provide an adequate container for the deeper questions that are inevitable on the inner journey. For such private spirituality to mature a communal aspect becomes necessary, as it is essential for that person to interact with other like-minded souls.

- *I believe but I don't belong.* A fundamental need of every human being is to have a sense of belonging. Believing and belonging are like two sides of the same coin. Believing by its nature can be quite nebulous and lacking direction Beliefs need to be tested, honed, lived out and enfleshed in the context of Christian community living.

THE ENDURING LEGACY

One hundred and fifty years of that particular brand of Romanised Catholicism so vehemently denounced by Kavanagh has left an enduring legacy that forms part of our current crisis of faith and practice:

- Churches were designed during that period in a manner that promoted anonymity and allowed for the least possible social interaction. They were inadvertently anti-community where the focus was on Christ the head but away from his body. To this day many churchgoers keep their distance from each other so that there is little chance of relating to someone else and any sense of belonging is minimised.

- Religion came to be seen as something you practiced on Sundays and was separate from your life for the rest of the week. Religion was one thing while business was another!

- The Sanctuary was seen to be the 'holy place' and the priest's domain where he was expected to do everything. Laity involvement was minimal and when first introduced was often perceived as the priest not doing his job. It also meant that people occupied the back of the church out of a sense of unworthiness.

- Liturgies that lacked prayer and a sense of the Sacred. These were usually rigid and lifeless, without the spontaneity and creativity that only feminine energy can bring. Such practices contributed to boredom and the popular myth that the greatest need in the Irish Church was for shorter masses!

- A view of sexuality that was distorted by rejection, fear, guilt and shame. This directly contributed to the scandals and cover-ups of recent decades in relation to clerical sex abuse and widespread institutional abuse.

- Clerical leadership that often became equated with control and dominance, in contrast to true leadership which will always empower others to take ownership and responsibility and to be involved in decisions.

- Church choirs performing from a distance, while participation by the congregation as an integral part of worship is neglected. In many churches it has become non-existent.

- The enduring legacy for today is undoubtedly an ageing population of churchgoers largely devoid of youth who have voted with their feet and not experienced Catholicism as expressing the reality of Christ's words in John 10:10, 'I came that they may have life and have it to the full'.

To summarise – we have known more:

- Hurt than Healing.
- Suffering than Redemption.
- 'Churchianity' than Christianity.
- Religiosity than genuine religion.
- Religious practice than Spiritual awareness.
- Compliance than genuine obedience.
- The love of power than the power of love.
- Self-effort than the free gift of grace.
- Information than transformation.
- Splitting than integration.
- Deflection than reflection.
- Secrecy than truth and transparency.
- Leaders with power than empowering leadership.
- Experience of authority than the authority of experience.
- Denial of our humanity than treating it as sacred.
- Repression of sexuality than celebration of it.
- Being driven by fear than being drawn by love.
- Outward show and hypocrisy than sincerity of heart.
- Guilt than mercy and forgiveness.
- Focus on unworthiness than gift of righteousness.
- Denial of shadow than integration of it.
- Projection of shadow than ownership of it.
- Control and manipulation than freedom.
- Punishment than encouragement.
- Self-denial than self-celebration.
- Self-rejection than self-acceptance.
- Self-depreciation than self-esteem.
- Grief than resolution.
- Endurance of faith than enjoyment of it.
- Brutality than compassion towards outer and inner child.
- Traditionalism than Incarnationalism.

- Perfectionism than wholeness.
- Focus on original sin than original blessings.
- Blame than taking responsibility.
- Outlawing of emotions than emotional enjoyment.
- Glorification of struggle and self-effort than surrender.
- Clericalism than priesthood.
- Destruction than formation in religious life.
- Head than heart.
- Stagnation than spiritual growth.
- Condemnation and damnation than salvation.
- Morality than spirituality.

If Patrick Kavanagh were still around he would be likely to say that we have made an unholy and totally unnecessary mess of the Good News of Jesus Christ entrusted to us.

IN SEARCH OF A ROUND TABLE

With centuries of a hierarchical model of Church deeply engrained within us it is difficult to think outside that particular box and embrace the model proposed by Vatican II of the Church as 'The People of God'. How we might move from one model to the other finds expression is a poem by Church Lathrop with the above title, *In Search of a Round Table*. In it he speaks of the struggle involved in changing a long narrow church into a round table church and how painful it is for both people and tables. He uses words like, *sawing, redefining, redesigning, redoing* and *rebirthing,* all of which speak of pain and suffering. Yet it is from such death comes life, from dying comes rising.

In a round table model of church there would be no thrones and the only ruler would be the healer of hearts who was also the footwasher from Nazareth.

In such a church there would be no preferred seating, with no first and no last places.

There would be no climbing up the ecclesiastical ladder.

It would be a church where all would share equal dignity and respect.

There would be no spaces above or below.

No one could claim to be more or less important than anyone else.

At a round table all would share different roles and ministries of service.

None would be *apart* but all would be *a part*.

There would be no *them* and *us*.

All would share power but none would have power over anyone else.

At a roundtable fellowship happens as people see each other face to face.

In such a place of roundness all would be invited to wholeness and to food.

He concludes his poem by saying:

Roundtabling means being WITH, A PART OF, TOGETHER and ONE.
It means room for the Spirit and for disturbing profound peace for all.
We are called to be a Church, a people of God,
And if God calls us we are bound to follow.

PART 3

A FAITH EXPERIENCED

THE NEED FOR EVANGELISATION

In the Catholic tradition, even among the most devout and those who faithfully practice their faith, there is an alarming degree of spiritual immaturity and general ignorance pertaining to matters of faith. A younger generation of Irish are better educated than any before, yet their religious knowledge is almost non-existent. This too is part and parcel of our enduring legacy. The vast majority have never asked the serious questions of life and few even have a rudimentary knowledge of the scriptures upon which our faith is based. In Catholicism, since the Reformation, there was even a bias against the Bible because it was perceived to be 'Protestant'. Apart from bias, it was viewed with suspicion. The well-known radio presenter Marian Finucane cites the example of her grandfather who when he decided to read the Bible from cover to cover was warned by his wife that to do so would run the risk of losing his faith! Even where practice of the faith is widespread, experience is seriously lacking. Those who have journeyed from religious practice to spiritual experience are few and far between; they may have much to teach us if we listen to their stories and draw together some common strands:

I presumed that because I had passed through the traditional sacramental rites of passage that I was on the right track but I wasn't. My heart was still empty.

I thought that by trying to lead a good moral life and practicing my faith that I was doing all that was required. It still left me unfulfilled.

It was only when someone challenged me to surrender my life to Christ that I realised I had never done so or had never been offered the opportunity, and so had been missing out on that which was central to my faith experience.

For most of my life I had more of a relationship with Church than with Jesus Christ.

I had a form of religion that was totally devoid of power to bring about any real change in my life. I had some information but knew nothing about transformation.

From my childhood I had been given many answers but it was only after I started to experience spiritual awakening that I began to ask the questions.

CHRIST AS THE CORNERSTONE

The journey of coming to personal faith in Jesus Christ seems to be central in all the stories of renewal and awakening. The majority of these would have believed and paid lip service to the fact that Christ was the cornerstone of their faith and practice and yet looking back realised that he had not been central to their lives at all. The centrality of Christ in the whole faith edifice is well expressed in what is believed to be a true story:

> A wealthy businessman who travelled widely had the opportunity during his life to accumulate lots of very valuable pieces of artwork and paintings. As an avid art collector his reputation became widely known. These were displayed in his mansion and when he died, the auction of his collection attracted the attention of art dealers from far and wide. The only painting that no one seemed interested in was that of a young boy by an unknown artist which wasn't in great condition. Surprisingly, on the day of the auction this piece was the first to be put up for sale. Bidding was slow and no one seemed interested except the man's butler who started bidding with a single pound. He knew the painting to be that of his master's beloved son, who had died as a youth. There were no more offers and the auctioneer lowered his hammer. The solicitor immediately intervened and halted the auction. He said that on the deceased's instructions he was now required to publically read out the will. It stated that whoever bought the painting of the son that he loved would be the one to inherit all that he owned.

The painting was the key to the inheritance. Our spiritual inheritance is intrinsically linked to our relationship with Christ. In the words of St Paul's letter to the Ephesians 1:3, 'It is in Christ that we are blessed with *all* the spiritual blessings of Heaven'.

WHEN THE JUDGE IS MY FRIEND!

> A man who parked on double yellow lines was fined for his offence. He failed to pay and was summonsed to appear in court. When asked by a friend why he appeared so unconcerned about standing in court he replied, 'Why should I be worried when I know the judge as well as I do.'

Christianity is not a morality contest of staying between the lines. Unfortunately, it has often been presented as such. It is about having a personal relationship with the Judge and when our conscience does not condemn us we have no need to be afraid in his presence. (John 3:20) A genuine spirituality will lead to a very mature level of moral behaviour where we do something because it is right and not simply because we were told to do so.

A DANGEROUS PRESUMPTION

Facilitating people to come into a personal and vibrant relationship with Jesus Christ has to be the key for hope and renewal in our churches. For so long there has been a presumption that because someone was baptised and confirmed then he or she had made a personal commitment to Christ or that the conferring of the sacraments would act like a slow-release capsule of grace throughout their lives. If someone had been conferred with the sacraments, they were automatically regarded as being Christians. Experience and observation proves that this is not the case. For a gift to be effective it needs both a giver and a receiver. The gift of grace is freely given in the sacraments and so they do not need to be reconferred but in every case they do need to be consciously received by the recipient. Otherwise, the gift remains dormant in that person's life like an unopened parcel with its contents waiting to be revealed.

The traditional understanding of a sacrament is that it is an outward sign of inward grace. For a sacrament to be in any way effective and confer the grace it signifies, it has to be received in the context of faith. Much of current religious practice is cultural rather than faith-based. If an alternative welcoming ceremony were available for a new baby lots of couples would opt for that rather than for baptism. For so many, the sacraments of initiation are cultural rites of passage rather than important milestones on a faith journey. Likewise, church attendance at certain times of the year like Christmas and Easter may well be more a cultural rather than a faith phenomenon.

The experience of those who have journeyed into spiritual maturity is that they inevitably came to a crisis that was also a crossroads. There was a point in time when a decision became necessary as to which direction to take. Like the two disciples on the road to Emmaus in Luke 24: it had come to evening and the Lord, whom they had not recognised as he, accompanied them on the journey, appeared as if to go on, and they had to say, 'Lord, stay with us, the day is nearly over.' And as he did, they broke bread together and with burning hearts recognised him as having been so close all along when they thought he was so far away.

THE WONDERFUL LEGACY OF CHARISMATIC RENEWAL

Openness to Spirit

Two hands reaching upwards in openness and prayer, forming the shape of a dove, symbolically suggest the coming of the Spirit. The Charismatic Renewal Movement brought new hope and vitality into a jaded Church, particularly in the 1970s, 80s and 90s. It was like a breath of fresh air blowing through the ecclesiastical windows opened the previous decade by Pope John XXIII when he convened the Second Vatican Council. At the time, many understood the Movement to be like a small stream that would eventually bring hope and renewal into the mainstream Church. To a large extent this is what did happen. Many of the most committed believers of today can trace their spiritual awakening back to those days of prayer meetings and scripture studies. Lots of the hymns in use at present were first heard at those gatherings and in churches where there is a good level of liturgical freedom and creativity, the Renewal Movement's influence is still quite obvious.

At every level the Renewal Movement has waned: perhaps through lack of sound teaching it may have lost its way, and in some cases degenerated into what has been described as 'holy huddles of the like-minded'. However, something that deserves to be retained from those days is the period of spiritual initiation known as *Life in the Spirit Seminars* which culminated in a decision to open one's heart to the Lord, accepting him as Saviour and praying for a new outpouring of the Spirit. This public commitment was for so many the turning point in their lives which even forty years later they can look back on and recall in vivid detail. Like St John who, as an old man writing his gospel, could still remember not just the day and place of his encounter with Christ, but that it was about the fourth hour. (John 1:39)

A story from New York in the 1950s captures the essence of the seminar process of leading people into a place of surrender and trust:

An elderly immigrant couple called Mike and Kate, both of whom were illiterate, travelled home one night and stopped to listen to the Salvation Army Band playing some songs. The religion of their childhood had become a distant memory and over the years they had drifted away from the faith. An ancient spark became reignited and they remained to the end when an altar call was extended for anyone listening who wished to commit their lives to Christ and accept him as Lord of their lives. Both went forward. It had been a chance encounter and they went away on cloud nine. Still basking in the glow of his newfound faith, Mike went to a men's gathering for worship the following Sunday. Returning home it was obvious that his spirits had dropped and he looked crestfallen. Kate was very concerned and enquired what went wrong to have caused such a change of heart. Mike explained that in the meeting he felt an outsider because all the men wore a blue pullover with something written across the front and being unable to read he didn't know what it meant. Kate assured him that for the next meeting she would knit him exactly what he needed and quickly got to work.

When completed, the problem arose as to what was to be written on the front. With neither able to read or write all they could do was bow their heads and pray for guidance. Looking up they saw a sign being erected in a shop window opposite. Believing it to be the answer Kate copied it onto the pullover. After the next meeting Mike came home jubilant. So many had commented on his jumper and said that the inscription on the front was by far the best they had ever seen. Kate naturally was more than curious as to what it meant. 'Would you believe,' said Mike, 'it says, 'This business is now under new management.' For someone who had just committed his life to the Lord what more apt an inscription could there be.

Undoubtedly, after forty or so years, the format and content of such *Life in the Spirit Seminars* needs to be revised and updated. Particularly as when they were first written there was little or no understanding of personal development, the importance of self-acceptance or inner healing. However, they do provide a framework that could well be utilised to great advantage in evangelising those who may already have been sacramentalised. In other words, to enable them to benefit from the graces of the sacraments that they probably have already received.

THE IMPORTANCE OF SURRENDER

For many Catholics the 'Morning Offering' was an important part of their daily prayers. This was an act of consecration formulated in terms of offering prayers, thoughts, words and deeds of the day to the Lord. A blatant omission was the offering of oneself. The acceptance of Christ as Lord and allowing the business that is my life to come under 'new management' always involves an act of radical surrender. Up until this point, the part of us that is in control is the ego. The ego is the little 'I' that has its own power, beauty and purpose. It is what makes us get up in the morning; it is what makes us health and safety conscious; it is what makes us take steps towards self-improvement and self-development. However, it does like its independence and abhors the idea of surrender because it signifies its own death. It is the seed that does not want to die even though it is only in doing so that it can begin to bear fruit. So it masquerades itself under a thousand different guises. It will even assume a very acceptable religious persona just so long as the 'I' can hold centre stage and take the credit.

Some of these egotistical beliefs that we can be living out of are as follows:

- That I can save my soul.
- That I can change myself.
- That I can become more spiritual.
- That I by my struggle can make it happen.
- That I can hear what the Lord has to say.
- That I can earn or deserve God's love.
- That I will have to wait until I die to know God.
- That I can surrender fully to God.
- That I need to be more charitable.
- That I need to be a better Christian.
- That I need to pray more.
- That I need to have more self-worth.

If the 'I' could take the credit it would also receive the glory. Because these beliefs are so common it poses the big question: how much of our religious practice is actually ego-based rather than Christ-centred?

The ego also holds us back by keeping us bound to a negative belief system:

- That I am unworthy and too imperfect.
- That I am guilty and therefore undeserving.
- That I am inadequate and incomplete.
- That I have never amounted to anything.
- That I am too weak and vulnerable.
- That I have failed too often in the past.
- That I have to do something as opposed to be that which I am.
- That I have to be somebody as opposed to who I really am.

With all of the above belief systems the 'I' holds centre stage. Even the common belief that 'I' can surrender to God needs to be critically evaluated. If 'I' could then 'I' would take the credit. This is where the ego always seeks self-glorification. When Christ said in Luke 9:23, 'If anyone wants to be a follower of mine he/she must first die to self,' the 'self' referred to is clearly not the Self that is made in the image and likeness of God but rather the small self that we understand as the ego. The same message was expanded further when he said; 'What does it profit a person if he gains the whole world and suffers the loss of his (True) Self'. (Matt. 16:26)

TRUE SELF OR FALSE SELF?

As Christians we believe that Christ dwells in our hearts. Buddhists similarly believe that at the heart of each person lies the Buddha nature. The goal of enlightenment is to realise this Divine indwelling. In psychological language this corresponds to the True Self and so our journey towards its realisation is the spiritual path, irrespective of which language we care to use. How do we know whether we are living from our false self where the ego reigns supreme or from our True Self where Christ is Lord?

The True Self is characterised by:

- Surrender and ease, the false self by struggle and effort.
- Harmony and peace, the false self by being easily offended.
- Service without reward, the false self by needing recognition.
- Co-operation with others, the false self by competition.
- Letting be, the false self by needing to control.
- Acceptance of change, the false self by resistance.

- Inner security, the false self by addictive behaviour.
- Living the present, the false self by being in the past or future.
- Self-compassion, the false self by guilt and unworthiness.
- Freedom of spirit, the false self by burden and heaviness.
- Adventure and excitement, the false self by fear and caution.
- Wonder and awe, the false self by boredom and routine.
- Content with being, the false self by compulsive doing.
- Relating with others, the false self by reacting to others.
- Detached attachment, the false self by fear and holding on.
- Peace and wellbeing, the false self by stress and anxiety.
- Being at home with silence, the false self by needing noise.
- Inner life and joy, the false self by outer dependencies.
- Comfortable with not knowing, the false self by needing certitudes.
- Self-expression, the false self by self-consciousness.
- Humour and being able to laugh at itself, the false self by seriousness.
- Inclusivity, the false self by them and us.
- Being real, the false self by needing designer labels.
- Gratitude and contentment, the false self by always wanting more.

CROSS – THE PLACE OF TRANSFORMATION

The central symbol of Christianity is undoubtedly the Cross. It is significant that the ego is clearly visible on the Cross as the vertical beam. It is the 'I' that has undergone the experience of dying only to be raised to a new level. Its energy has been transformed into spirit energy. The Cross therefore represents in psychological terms the ego in proper relation to the True Self or in spiritual terms the small self that has surrendered in order for the Christ Self to be manifest. In other words, for Christ to take centre place the ego has to be transformed. The very process of suffering, death and resurrection is in fact the displacement and death of ego and also its continued existence at a deeper level in what we call resurrection life.

LETTING GO AND LETTING GOD – THE KEY TO ABUNDANCE.

What sets Christianity apart from all the other great world religions is that it represents God's search for us while all the others are about our search for God. With Christianity, the initiative is all on the Divine side. This means that the Christian life was never meant to be one enormous effort to be loved by God but rather one great act of gratitude for being loved so totally and unconditionally. In the words of St Paul, we work *out* our salvation in fear and trembling. We do not have to work *for* it as if it all depended on us.

The key word in the Christian story is *Incarnation*: God becoming man and taking on human form. It is about God opening his heart and stretching out his arms to the world. This is the message of Christmas expressed in the babe with open arms and also the message of Christ's life as he stretched out his arms eventually to have them nailed that way on the Cross.

The most famous verse in the Bible also sums up the Christian message that, 'God so loved the world that he gave his only begotten Son so that all who believe in him would not be lost but have eternal life'. (John 3:17) In other words his love was not the greedy type that wanted to hold on but the generous type that let go.

For years, those in addiction recovery have preached the message, 'Let go and let God.' This is what lies at the heart of Christ's teaching and what we might so easily overlook is that it is also the key to abundance.

The oldest Christian hymn in existence is found in St Paul's letter to the Philippians. (Phil. 2:9–16) It is believed to be much older than his writings and expresses the mind of Christ:

> *Though he was in the form of God, Jesus did not cling to his equality with God as something to be grasped after. Instead he emptied himself and became as all men are, and being as men are he humbled himself and assumed the condition of a slave.*

> *Because of this God raised him on high and gave him the name that is above all other names so that at the name of Jesus every knee should bend and every tongue confess that Jesus Christ is Lord, to the glory of God the Father.*

The two words that stand out in that hymn are; he did not *cling* and he did not *grasp*. Both of these words point towards a key word in Christian theology: *kenosis*, which means the self-emptying of Christ. It was his journey of life that led through the Cross to his exaltation. It was also the central message of his life – in both words and deeds – to his followers. He invited the fishermen to leave their nets and the tax collectors their posts. Later, he would invite the rich young man to leave his wealth and so many to leave their former lifestyle. To all who wanted the abundance of eternal life he first invited them to let go. Not all were prepared to accept the challenge; some went away sad but for those who were prepared to open their hands they had also opened their hearts to the experience of abundance. This was the assurance offered by Jesus to his disciples when he told them that, 'Anyone who has left father or mother, houses or land for my sake or for the sake of the Gospel will receive a hundredfold in this life and in the age to come eternal life.' (Luke18:27–30) The act of letting go is the key to abundant living. In Christian terms, this is what we would call the grace-filled life.

LIVING LIFE WITH OPEN HANDS

Letting Go

Christ's basic teaching about the importance of letting go is written into the very fabric of our existence. When we come into the world as a baby our hands are tightly closed. When our time comes to leave they open out. The time in-between is about learning the art of letting go. From having been present with so many at the time of their passing it is obvious that there are varying qualities in the way people let go and die. For some it seems that life is taken from them while for others they graciously give up their spirit. It would appear that those who hold on in life still hold tight onto the end while those who live life with open hands are most ready to let go in death. This attitude of just letting go is expressed in the following story:

> An old sailor was dying when someone asked him how he was preparing for his final voyage. He replied that he was bundling together all the bad things he had done in life and also all the good things and he was in the process of throwing them overboard so as to be free to drift to glory on the plank of God's mercy.

HOLDING ON AND LETTING GO – EXERCISE

A little exercise that can be quite informative is to imagine yourself holding tightly onto something you value. Someone wants to take it from you and you are unwilling to let go. Under threat you then tighten your grip all the more. Notice both how you feel and also your body posture.

Now reverse the exercise. Imagine that you are giving or letting go of something. You are able and willing and so there is no resistance. Once again notice your body posture and how that stance makes you feel.

In the first case you were witnessing exactly what Christianity is not all about, while in the second you were touching on what lies at the core of Christ's message.

There are so many things worth noting in what you have just done:

When you were holding on did you notice just how tense your body felt, how your breathing had become restricted, and when you were letting go just how relaxed you were?

When holding on tight, did you notice how isolated and closed in you were on yourself, and then when you opened up and your hands extended out, how easy it was to reach out and touch – which is where community begins. We make a very small parcel when we get too wrapped up in ourselves!

Notice that when you were holding on how dour your facial expression had become whereas when you opened up smiling came naturally and if you had been doing this exercise with a group it might even have been contagious.

Finally, did you notice that the tighter you held on, the more your eyes closed and the more you let go, the wider they opened? If you pardon the pun there's more to that than meets the eye because the more we close down, all we can see are scarcity and need. It's only as we let go that we are free to see and receive abundance and blessing. When closing down on ourselves the focus goes inwards and we find ourselves looking into a bottomless pit of needs and wants that absolutely nothing is capable of filling.

Here we discover that letting go is not a moral issue but a visionary tool because as we see so do we create. It is our thoughts that are always creating our reality. To think scarcity is to be in want whereas to think abundance is being ready to receive from the hand of providence.

> One day a little boy got his hand stuck in an earthenware jar and no one could get it out. Along came a stranger who offered to help. Taking him aside it took him scarcely a few moments to free the hand. Everyone was amazed and questioned what he had done. 'It was quite simple,' he replied, 'I just offered him five euro instead of the twenty cents coin he was holding onto.'

It is so easy to be just like the little boy; holding onto so little, our hands are not open to receive so much. When it comes to holding on we all have our own issues, whether it be our fears or worries about the future or our guilt and regrets in relation to the past.

Parents can hold on too tightly to their children and partners can be far too possessive of their spouses. The jealousy that destroys so many relationships is like a dragon that devours love under the pretext of keeping it alive.

WHO AM I?

Mystery Box

Inside the mystery box is a shell containing a pearl. This is symbolic of the pearl of great price that is the True Self. Before the box can be opened it appears as a conundrum because inside is the key that is necessary to unlock it. A lot of moves are necessary before discovering the right ones that release the key; all of which is symbolic of finding out who we really are and the discovery that all that we search for is already within.

> *A wealthy businessman bought a costly diamond in Madras in India. He proceeded to board a train bound for Delhi. A pickpocket who had seen him purchase the diamond followed him and took a seat in the same compartment. On the long journey, as the businessman slept, the pickpocket searched again and again for the diamond, but in vain; it was nowhere to be found. Utterly frustrated he decided to come clean with his fellow passenger about who he was and what his intentions were. The businessman*

smiled and said, 'I know. I saw you watching and knew what you were up to when you followed me on board so I made sure to carefully hide away the diamond and in a place you would never think of looking. It's inside your own pocket!'

The deepest and most basic of all human questions is 'Who am I?' It is our identity quest that becomes more urgent as we get older. In the first half of life we had goals that were of necessity ego-directed. We had to get educated; find our place in the world; take on a job; probably get married and become a parent. We adopted certain roles in order to survive. However, we are always greater than any roles we adopt and they do not constitute our total identity.

The second half of life is characterised by a different kind of journey that is less outer orientated and more inner directed towards the True Self. The beginning of this movement is often precipitated by a crisis, the normal mid-life crisis or a particular crisis that can happen at any age. This is why it is not uncommon to find in a young person a level of spiritual maturity that is way beyond his or her years. At some point of suffering an awakening has taken place and a depth dimension been established.

For the majority, by the time we reach mid-life, our roles and our identity have become quite overlapped. So we tend to define ourselves in terms of what we do, what we have, who we are in relationship with and what others think of us. We feel that we cannot do without these external aspects of our lives. Paradoxically it is only when we experience the pain of losing something that was dear to us that we even embark on the exciting journey of Self-discovery. Our roles change as we get older and unless we learn to separate what we do from who we are we cannot even cross the threshold into this mysterious world of Self and authentic spirituality.

As a general guide, whatever words we are most inclined to place immediately after the statement 'I am' offers the clue as to where our role and identity have become confused and overlapped. Some common examples might be:

I am not what I do. It is but my role. At the same time I may do what I am as an expression of my uniqueness. The myth here is that 'I am only as good as I am useful.' An over identification with role makes redundancy or retirement almost impossible to cope with.

I am not what I have. To have more does not necessarily mean to be more. It is possible to have everything and still feel empty. To build my house on material things is always to build on the foundation of sand. One minute in a doctor's surgery receiving news of a serious diagnosis can change a lifetime of perspective on what is truly important.

I am not my body. I only live in it and one day will cast it aside. Medical science teaches that the cells of our bodies completely renew themselves every seven years so we have already outlived our bodies many times in the course of our lifetime. My body is like a pet that has to be carefully looked after but to identify myself with it makes death seem like utter annihilation and the grave our final home. To remind myself of this truth when undergoing an unpleasant medical procedure or even on a visit to the dentist can be most effective.

I am not my age or appearance. This is to buy into the myth expressed in the words of the song, 'You have to be young and beautiful if you want to be loved'. If, having been identified with appearance for decades, I now see my parent looking back at me in the mirror I may, out of fear, try to defy the ageing process. To graciously accept what is allows the ageless beauty of the True Self to shine through.

I am not someone's partner. Co-dependency is endemic in society where people define themselves as the wife or husband of so and so. Living my life through someone else I lose connection with my own centre. Making another the light of my life is to leave myself in darkness and not free to follow my individual path.

I am not someone's mother or father. Parents who hold onto their role for too long and fail to let go of their children stand in real danger of losing altogether that which they hold most dear. Self-hood begins in the going away and love is proved in the letting go. Adult children who do not properly separate from their parents still need to be fostered in marriage because psychologically they have never really left their father or mother.

I am not what others think of me. Addiction approval makes me look to others for validation while it also prevents me from being true to myself. A liberating motto to live by is, 'What other people think of me is none of my business.'

I am not my past with its mistakes and regrets. To over identify with my past is to make everyday a yesterday. I need humility to be self-forgiving and offer to myself the alms of my own compassion.

I am not a helpless victim. To visit a fortune teller in order to find out what is going to happen in the future is to express the belief of being a victim. The opposite is to assume responsibility for my life where by changing my thoughts and making the proper choices I create my own reality. The alternative is to B-lame!

I am not my suffering. To become identified with my suffering also means that I slip into the victim mode and fuelled by self-pity will tend to create even more for myself. In a strange way it is possible to enjoy bad health! Could this be why Christ asked the question of so many who were ill, 'Do you really want to be healed'? To be healed meant to assume responsibility and no longer be a helpless victim.

I am not my thoughts. Identification with thought is firmly rooted in Descartes' philosophy, 'I think therefore I am'. Perhaps of all our inherited false identifications this is the worst. We have cultivated our minds but at the expense of our hearts. Because of this the Christian Church still suffers so much from emotional sterility and lack of connectedness to the wellsprings of our essential humanity.

I am not my education or lack of it. In a society that so highly values education it is easy to place value on myself in relation to the standard reached and to forget that my intrinsic worth is something totally separate. We don't get there by degrees!

The above represent but a few of the many false identifications that we unwittingly fall prey to. It might appear that if we are none of the above then we are dead, while paradoxically we are never more alive. An essential part of our *kenosis* or self-emptying has to be the letting go of all that we are not in order to discover the greatness of who we really are. In the words of Psalm 139, 'We are fearfully, wonderfully made.' This detachment inevitably involves suffering. While we can name all that we are not, our true identity is always shrouded in mystery and defies definition. Yet, in the end it simply is and remains the most real thing that there is. Discovering our true identity is to be amazed at the wonder of our own magnificence.

MEDITATION

Meditation and reflection are often confused. Reflection is the mental process of reviewing one's life, pondering over an event or slowly reading a sacred text. It is a mental process even if the heart is involved, whereas meditation is the process of becoming detached from the world of thought. The end result is not to become a non-thinking being but rather to allow the head to find its home in the heart and allow our thoughts to flow from that space where the two have become integrated. When making the spinning top shown I encountered a problem: it was not balanced and failed to spin until I reduced the head size. It was a wonderful insight into the practice of meditation.

Spinning Top

Meditation is an inner journey from the ego to the True Self where we begin to realise that our lives are not just a drop *in* the ocean but are a drop *of* the ocean; we are not separate but part of all that is.

Meditation facilitates a growing realisation that nothing outside of myself can offer me any more than what I already have within myself. It is to discover the treasure hidden in the field of Self or the Kingdom that is within.

Meditation is to begin drawing from my own inner well of infinite resources rather than always going to outer wells with unrealistic expectations. It is to be like the Woman of Samaria in John 4 who came to draw water with her bucket but went home with the well.

With such widespread interest in meditation at present, there is no end to the methods available. Many of these are somewhat complex. Here is a simple one that I use myself which I find invaluable.

THE PLACE OF NOWHERE

Sitting comfortably with your eyes closed, imagine that on the left side of your mind is a screen with another on the right side. Take a prayer like the 'Our Father' and imagine the word 'Our' appearing on the left screen. Spend a few moments looking at it and then focus on the other screen and see the word 'Father'. Again spend some time just looking but without analysing. Next shift your focus to the space in-between, the empty space and rest awhile.

Again return to the left screen and look at the word 'who' appearing and take a few moments before turning to the right screen and seeing the word 'art'. Then come back to the centre and just be present in the empty space, the place of nothingness.

Once again repeat the exercise, this time seeing on the left screen the word 'in' and slowly moving right to the other screen with the word 'Heaven'. Again come back to the in-between space: the place of emptiness, the place of nothingness and this time simply be there, at home with yourself and with all that is.

The space in-between is also the place of NOWHERE which can also be looked at as NOW-HERE. We are never more present than when we are in the place of nowhere. In contrast, much of the time in our so-called busyness the question could be asked, 'If you didn't know where you were right now, where would you be'? Just being physically present is no guarantee of real presence.

ACCEPTANCE OF WHAT IS

Going With The Flow

The piece of sculpture depicted is of two circles that are so connected as to form an endless circle. Going with the flow in the smaller circle, even when it appears to be going backwards, always brings us back into the greater. When we say that someone has taken the path of least resistance it means that he or she has taken the lazy way out. However, the spiritual path is truly the way of least resistance because that which we resist will always persist. From the cradle to the grave, change is an inevitable part of life. It is not change itself that causes so much suffering but rather our resistance to it. Learning to go with the flow is an important key to experiencing inner peace and wellbeing. When adverse circumstances arise we usually resist and resent them. It is in their acceptance that either we change or we get the strength to surmount them. Similarly, with negative emotions we so easily try to block their unwelcome intrusion. In allowing them to simply be we treat them as welcome guests and find that in the words of the poet Rumi in his poem, *The Guest House,* they come bearing unexpected gifts. Here the Buddhist wisdom has much to teach us as to how to deal with reality: 'It is as it is so how can we deal with it best?' Or to rephrase, 'Things are as they are; how can we make the most of them?'

The wisdom of addiction counselling to *Let go and let God* is brought to a deeper level with the *Going with the Flow* piece. It suggests not only to *Let go and let God* but also to *Let go of the way we think things should be going.* Such an approach can transform our prayer life and truly let God be God. It is our disappointment with God when he does not take our advice that can cause us so much grief.

THE TRANSFORMATION CHALLENGE

Pen Holder and Ornate Bowl

Pictured on the left is a piece of shipwreck from two hundred years ago. It was recovered from the seabed and bears the marks of centuries beneath the sea. On the right is an Ornate Rose Bowl. Inserted in the bit of wreckage are a penholder and a pen. The primary vocation of every person is to be authentic, to become our own unique selves. The word authentic comes from the word 'author'. It suggests that the truly authentic person is one who has taken hold of the pen and is authoring the script that is their life. In other words it is someone who is not allowing others or circumstances to define who they are. This is the movement from seeing oneself as a victim of life to taking responsibility for my life. It is recognising that I am a co-creator of my future by virtue of the thoughts I think, the actions I take and the choices I make.

Life by its nature presents us with lots of wreckage; losses, setbacks and disappointments are part of the human condition. They are, in the words of Shakespeare, 'The slings and arrows of outrageous fortune.' The challenge is what to do with what happens. Do we spend our lives bemoaning our losses or can we see them as raw material for building better lives. The Rose Bowl is made from the same raw material as the piece of shipwreck. It can be the wreckage of life – the childhood trauma, the failed marriage, the broken heart – that carries the potential for some of the most exquisite beauty to be created. The big choice is whether to stay with the wreckage or to make something of it.

> *Can a man grow from the dead clod of failure,*
> *Some consoling flower.*
> *Something humble as a dandelion or a daisy*
> *Something to wear as a buttonhole in Heaven*

Patrick Kavanagh – 'From Failure Up'

OUR IMAGE OF GOD

The following four stories illustrate very clearly that our image of God and consequently our faith life are intrinsically linked to childhood experience of our parents:

> *A religious sister who all her life had enjoyed a very easy and natural relationship with God could easily attribute it to her relationship with her father. Growing up in a small town in the West of Ireland, she remembered the old-style Redemptorists priests coming to give a parish mission with their message of hellfire and damnation. Their sermons were so fear-based at the time that many thought they were going to Hell. Before going to the mission their father called his two daughters aside and had a word with them. 'Listen to what the priests are saying but don't take everything to heart. They have to be saying something and most of what they say will be forgotten by next week. Just remember this one thing: I am your father and there is nothing that you have ever done and absolutely nothing that you will ever do for which I have not already forgiven you. And that's because I am your father. Now think about this: Jesus told you to call God your Father.'*

Having taken her father's message to heart it became the foundation for her faith in a loving and infinitely merciful God and was also the key to living a very fulfilling life.

> *A similar insight comes from a lady who claimed to have lived an almost guilt-free life in spite of having made her share of mistakes. She said very tellingly that, 'In my father's eyes I could do no wrong'.*

The truth of being forgiven from before we even sin is expressed in John 13 where Jesus washed his disciples' feet. Peter is surprised and asks, 'Lord, are you going to wash my feet?' Jesus answers, 'You will not realise now what I am doing but later you will understand.' Not long after, Jesus is arrested and Peter is suspected of being one of his followers. When put to the test he denies his association three times and even takes an oath that he does not know the man. It is then that a cock crows and Peter hangs his head in shame. At this point, as he is looking down at his feet, the significance of having had those feet washed must have dawned. Jesus had already forgiven him and this was the reassurance he needed to forgive himself and later substitute his three denials with a threefold expression of love.

> *In contrast to the above stories, another woman said that her image of God was of, 'Someone whose expectations of her were so high and whose opinion of her was so low that she felt that she always lived under his frown.' It wasn't God she was really talking about but how she had experienced her own father.*

Finally, there's the story of a very scrupulous man who worked as a prison warden. His life was completely governed by rules and regulations and any deviation from the straight and narrow was enough to convince him that he would go to Hell. He described his father as someone who, 'God, man or the devil couldn't please.' Coming home from school he never knew what to expect and the slightest misdemeanour was enough to provoke his outrage and dole out the harshest of punishment. As an adult, his image of God was still that of his father.

GOD OF LOVE OR JUSTICE?

Many, from an older generation in particular, have great difficulty balancing the idea of God's justice with his love. Having being reared on a God of Justice, who took strict account of all our wrongdoings, they understandably feel that the Church has gone soft on sin in its preaching and teaching about God as love. If God is all love then do we have any need to be concerned about sin in our lives? One obvious truth is that we live in a moral universe where we don't just break the commandments but we break ourselves on them. There are consequences to our actions and to a large extent our life's experience is a reflection of the choices we have made whether for good or bad. A sentence that may be helpful in understanding how both the love of God and the justice of God lie at the heart of our human experience is:

God remembers until we remember, and when we remember, God forgets.

A way of understanding what is being expressed here is to draw on our psychological understanding of the nature of repression and denial. This would attest to the issues of life, either what we have done or what has been done to us, once consigned to the unconscious, do not become dormant but continue to control our lives in a myriad of ways that could be understood as judgments. To lock away any part of life's experience is to bury not just an unpleasant event but also a bundle of energy that is necessary in order to live life to the full. The psychiatrist Carl Jung's understanding of sin was, 'To remain in a state of unconsciousness.' This is to live in a state of unawareness where, without self-knowledge, we live a shallow existence and mostly react rather than relate to life. Relating is what we do in the present while reacting comes from the past; it is a re-enactment of an old scenario or feeling that has long been supressed. Reactions do not convey the truth of any situation; another may see it quite differently, but they do tell us what we may least want to hear but most need to know about ourselves in order to grow and mature. It is our reactions of hurt, anger, rejection, greed, etc. that constitute so much 'sin' in our lives. Because of this, learning to monitor our reactions as an examination of conscience can become an invaluable tool in uncovering the truth that has the power to bring us freedom. Until we remember it would seem that God remembers; the truth of our lives is inescapable.

The apocryphal Gospel of Thomas has a piece of challenging wisdom in Logion 70 where it states:

> *Bring forth that which is within you*
> *And that which is within will save you.*
> *If you fail to bring forth that which is within*
> *That which is within will destroy you.*

This particular translation of the ancient text seems to capture the essential truth of the necessity to bring into the light of consciousness all that is buried in the darkness of the unconscious. It forms part of the movement from darkness into light or being 'born again'. Bringing into form and fullness the True Self, the image of the Divine that lies at the heart of our being, is the spiritual path. Failure to engage in the process therefore becomes 'Self' destructive.

Whatever is brought to the light of consciousness is exposed to God's mercy and so can be transformed. Once secure in his redeeming love, we can then have the reassurance that God forgets.

HEALING AND INTEGRATION

It is obvious from the gospels that healing played a central role in Christ's ministry. On so many pages we find him either coming from healing someone, engaged in healing or on his way to heal. His healing miracles were signs of the Kingdom that awakened faith in those who witnessed them. In so many examples we find that there was a progression involved for the individual, of not just being healed, but becoming whole; the miracle was not always instantaneous. Mark 2:1–11 contains the story of a paralysed man being let down through the roof and placed in front of Jesus by his friends. Jesus' first response was to say, 'Your sins are forgiven,' to be followed by, 'Take up your bed and walk.' Was this man paralysed by guilt; was his physical condition the expression of his inner state? The implication certainly is there, and undoubtedly guilt can immobilise us and prevent our moving forward in life. While making us live in the past it robs us of hope for the future and fills our lives with misery in the present. Perhaps it can also make us sick?

When our bodies become ill our immediate desire is to regain health. We forget that this particular discomfort may be an invitation to become whole. Our body may be expressing something that we have not been saying or have not been able to say or it may be an indication of a lifestyle imbalance. So we treat the symptom and in overlooking the cause we miss the message. To ask the question, 'What is this illness trying to teach me?' is to co-operate with it as a friend who is there for me rather than treat it as an enemy who wants to destroy me. This rather radical and yet compassionate approach to sickness seems to be an essential part of the gospel message. Even with minor conditions that make us take time out we are advised to, 'Take care of ourselves'. The underlying message is that prior to this we were somewhat out of balance and *not* taking enough care, especially of our *Self*.

Another of the many stories where a progression was involved in healing is found in Mark 3:1–5: the story of the man with the withered hand. Here Jesus enters the synagogue and notices a man whose hand has been withered from birth. This was likely to be someone who did not want to be seen and who always kept in the background. His handicap was probably a source of embarrassment and in not wanting to draw attention to it had kept himself in the shadows. The first stage of the healing process is where Jesus calls him to come out in front. For someone who had been hiding all his life this was a major step forward and a symbolic move towards self-acceptance. As challenging as it was for the individual to respond to that invitation the next must have been far greater: Jesus asks him to, 'Stretch out his hand'. This seems simple but for someone habitually wearing long sleeves in order to hide the source of his shame and embarrassment it demanded real faith. The very thing he most wanted to hide he was now being asked to reveal. In response to his doing so his hand was healed and Jesus was able to say, 'Your faith has saved you.' The word *saved* also implies becoming whole, coming as it does from the Latin word *salus* meaning wholeness. The story therefore is so much more than one about a withered hand being healed but more importantly about a man becoming whole and able to stand out and take his proper place in the world.

SPIRITUALITY – THE ART OF HOMECOMING

Russian Dolls

The set of Russian dolls provide a very useful visual aid for the process of integration. Each doll has its place in the larger and forms an essential part of the whole. A case study where some non-essential details have been changed provides an insight as to how each part of the personal and family story needs to be acknowledged and restored to its rightful place:

A man in his mid-fifties was forced to take time out from work because of bullying. He was a man of strong build and muscular appearance so hearing that he was a victim came as a surprise. He described how for years he felt as if he were empty on the inside and needing to fill that space with whatever came along, like working long hours, accumulating material possessions and engaging in transient relationships. No longer able to work, his main escape route had been cut off and he was in crisis.

When asked the question, 'What age would you be if you didn't know what age you were,' he very quickly replied, 'About thirteen.' At that age he had a major skin problem; received constant bullying and been dubbed the 'Leper'. The present difficulty had awakened that earlier period of his life with all the feelings that he thought he had locked away. It was as if that painful period was like a sub-personality that was now superimposing itself on his adult experience. When asked if he had spoken about his earlier difficulties he said that in his home he was never listened to and didn't have a voice. In particular he felt that his father always preferred his elder brother and had never shown any interest in him. This behaviour also needed to be examined as to what was really going on. Not long before he was conceived another brother had died at two years old. His father, more so than his mother, had buried his feelings and never spoke about the loss. However, this became the legacy for the next born. Not only could the man in question never be the son that died, but also his father, because of the earlier emotional wound, always kept his distance out of fear of being hurt again.

As the story unfolded some key insights emerged:

t was not because there was anything wrong with him that his father was unable to get close, but he did need to forgive him for being so emotionally unavailable.

As a child he was deeply hurt and felt angry that his brother was preferred. He now recognised how in adult life he was still comparing himself with other men and never feeling good enough.

The skin eruptions of his early teens he could understand to be his body's way of expressing the anger that he was carrying.

As an adult he was now able to recognise how his anger was still leaving him vulnerable and getting him into trouble. Also, that he was responsible for his victimhood by virtue of what was going on in himself.

While he was apparently being haunted by his past, these aspects of his life were seeking integration. Each one was sacred and essential for his wholeness.

As the different layers of the story emerged they were like different parts of the Russian Doll with each one asking to be brought back home. With insight, awareness and some visual imagination exercises, he emerged very quickly from his crisis with a real sense of integration and having welcomed back home the estranged parts of himself. What began as a breakdown had become a breakthrough of what he had held all his life in the darkness of unawareness. So much of him had been 'born again.

'When I loved myself enough, the neglected, rejected and dejected parts of myself, the orphans of my soul, came together in seamless unity and that was the beginning of finding inner peace.'

Kim McMillen

RELATIONSHIPS – RELATING OR REACTING?

The Freedom to Be – In Relationship

The Bible has been described as God's love letter to his people. It abounds with references to love. 'Love one another as I have loved you.' (John 15:12) 'By this shall all people know that you are my disciples, that you have love for each other.' (John 13:34) The quality of our lives is determined, not by what we achieve, or what we have, but by the quality of our relationships. It is in relation to others that we grow, blossom, mature and find the courage to reach for our potential. As we journey through life we are either moving towards isolation or intimacy. Intimacy can be understood as, *Into me you may see*; it is about allowing others to see into our inner world. Isolation is where we become closed down and gradually come to live in a world with a population of just one, and even that can feel crowded!

The word relationship implies the ability to relate and just because people interact in close proximity, or live together, doesn't mean that they are actually relating; it may amount to far more reacting than relating. While we relate in the present we react from the past. Reacting is a re-enactment of old unresolved issues that have never been integrated in our lives. Our reactions do not give us the truth of a situation since someone else may see it quite differently. What they do give us is the truth about ourselves; what we may least want to hear but most need to know, if we are to become whole. The problem when we react is that we also regress emotionally to the age we were when the original hurt took place. This is why we so easily become irrational and over the top since we are seeing the situation not as it is but as we are. Reactions can also get us into serious trouble especially when the original trauma took place at a pre-rational age in our development. A man carrying the wound of abandonment as a baby could be capable of murdering the woman that he loves and spend the rest of his life wondering what 'possessed' him to do it. The word 'possessed' is probably the most accurate description of what took him over in that moment of madness where in blind rage he had no rationale for what he was doing nor the ability to consider the consequences. Our perception of reality becomes seriously distorted when viewed through the lens of our reactions.

Having the freedom to be in relationship requires a level of maturity whereby we have acknowledged and integrated our past issues at least to the extent that they no longer undermine our ability to relate in the present. The American writer Marianne Williamson captures the essence of this truth when she says, *'If we don't bring healing to the child that we were, the adult we want to become doesn't stand a chance.*

Dancer inside Light Bulb

When we first share a secret, expose a deep wound or revisit an old trauma with another person, it tends to be extremely difficult, especially if has caused us shame. The real difficulty is not always talking to the other but rather admitting the truth to myself. Until them we probably felt as if we were the only person in the whole world who has this problem and to a certain extent that is true. In our bubble of isolation, like the dancing girl inside the light bulb, we are the only one. Yet when we find someone trustworthy, who will respect what we say, and open our heart to them, the old saying becomes true that, 'A trouble shared is a trouble halved'. After the initial disclosure to one it becomes so much easier to talk to others and there may come a time when the same story will be told in front of a group as a testimony of recovery with everyone applauding. When this happens others are being empowered and encouraged to tell their story. The personal has now become part of the universal story of struggling humanity where we are all made of the same stuff but cooked somewhat different!

Maria was a separated parent who was having major difficulties with her eldest son Mark to the point where they could easily have become estranged for life. When asked who he reminded her of she admitted that it was her husband with whom she had a very acrimonious breakup. Mark, she said, was just like him. Her anger, still unresolved from that time, was now being displaced on her son who carried his own hurt from his parents' breakup. She came to realise that she was expecting a positive response from someone she was quite negative towards. In effect she was getting back what she was giving out and reaping what she was sowing. Once Maria could see where she needed to change, her son began to respond in a remarkably different manner.

In his work situation Tony found his supervisor impossible to cope with. He felt treated with disrespect and criticised at every possible opportunity. Again when asked whom did she remind him of, he looked surprised and said, 'Actually, my eldest sister – why did I not see that; she never forgave me for being born.' He was surprised that he had never thought of such an obvious connection but now could see why this lady had the power to make him feel so small and why he didn't have the inner strength to be assertive with her. Then another insight followed where he remembered this same girl having remarked that she had a younger brother that she never liked and had no time for. Two childhood dramas were being re-enacted each day in the workplace.

Not long after retiring Rita had developed a hearing problem in her left ear. She admitted that for some time she had been listening to verbal abuse coming from a former friend who would ring her at unacceptable times, often late into the night. For some reason she was unable to stand up to this woman and a friend was able to point out that all her life she had been listening to abuse from female bosses and had never been able to say 'No' and assert herself. The first person to level abuse and constantly criticise her was her mother. This took the form of, 'Why can't you do this or that?' or 'Why do you dress like you do?' and frequently, 'Why can't you be more like so and so?' There seemed to be little or no warmth in the mother and were the child to speak out for herself it could easily incur even more rejection and would be felt like annihilation. With such early wounds, Rita's life began to follow a pattern where with so many subsequent female relationships she was unable to use her voice as a result of the same fear of being wiped out.

Life is not always one darn thing after another.
It is more often the same darn thing over and over!

One sacrament that has great potential to bring healing into people's lives is marriage. It is in the interaction of two people on a daily basis that all earlier issues will sooner or later raise their heads for attention and demand healing. A nine-year-old schoolgirl was asked what love was. With wisdom beyond her years she replied, 'It's the first feeling that you feel before the bad stuff gets in the way.' When a couple get married they inevitably come to the relationship carrying two suitcases from their past. These are made up of ancestral and parental influences along with any unresolved issues from earlier relationships. Sooner, rather than later, these suitcases will be opened permanently and both parties will need to find a place for the contents. Where they fail to integrate their past issues these become projected, or dumped, onto each other. Unmet needs from childhood get carried forward with the person they are now closest to being forced to carry them. Such expectations tend to be resentments under construction because no one can meet the needs that each is responsible for meeting themselves.

When a couple speak of their needs not being met in the marriage, nearly always it will be those same needs that were not met in childhood. This is where there is so much truth in the saying that, 'In every marriage bed there are six people': apart from the couple there's his and her parents as well. In particular it will be his relationship with his mother that will have a huge bearing on how he relates to his wife and similarly it will be her relationship with her father that will greatly influence her relationship with her husband. Jealousy, possessiveness and overdependency are directly related to childhood insecurities. The relationship that begins with two people coming together as adults can quickly regress into parent–child mode where he relates to her as mother and she to him as father. When this happens a couple invariably find themselves at cross purposes.

> *Tom and Joan were both in their mid-sixties and married for nearly forty very turbulent years. In spite of all the bickering some deep love had kept them together but their conflict was almost unbearable for their four children as they grew up. For some reason they had never related what they were experiencing to what had gone on in the past. He reacted strongly when his wife came across as domineering and bossy as his mother had been. She on the other hand couldn't cope when he got angrybecause as a child she had grown up terrified of her father's anger, especially when he lost his temper with her. For this couple the situation didn't come right overnight, but with a growing awareness as to when the relationship dynamic from adult–adult to parent–child, had changed and with each party integrating their past, peace and harmony began to reign.*

In the above stories a common and surprising truth emerges. All of the parties were reacting rather than relating, with none having awareness as to why they were doing so. Even the most basic questions like, 'Where might this problem be coming from?' or 'Who does this person you have difficulty with remind you of?' had never been asked. Each one was suffering from a blind spot that was so apparent to someone else and yet so hidden to themselves. Something may be as 'plain as the nose on our face' and yet we never see our nose directly. It is only as we allow our truth to be reflected back by another that our blind spots can be eliminated and then we can begin to truly relate as we grow in insight.

THE HEALING OF ABUSE

The Deep Wound

The vase made from yew contains a heart shaped feature. This was originally a defect, a rotten part, that took extra care and attention in order to be integrated into the overall design and so transformed into a feature. The experience of sexual abuse is a dreadful violation that cuts to the core of who I am as a person. It is a wound that cannot be eliminated but it can be slowly transformed by being integrated.

Nothing in living memory, or even far beyond, has had such a devastating impact on the Institution of the Catholic Church as the recent and widespread abuse scandals. The degree of anger and outright rage felt in relation to this has been unprecedented. Both believers and non-believers alike have been shocked by the scale and nature of reaction of those who hold the levers of power in the Church. Too often they took the side of the accused over the accuser and appeared reluctant to hand evidence over to the lawful authorities. Too often they dimmed the light rather than direct it towards the darkness. Far too often they protected the interests of the institution rather than champion the rights of those who had been abused and bullied by representatives of the Church. The tendency for so long was to put a protective wall around the accused thereby abandoning and isolating the innocent.

In recent years setting up codes of practice around reporting procedures and the safeguarding of children have been given priority in every diocese. Learning to understand and provide an adequate response to these terrible disclosures has been a steep learning curve for both Church and State. Even the professionals in the field, who were often the advisors to those in office, have found their understanding of the subject to be quite inadequate.

Sigmund Freud, the founding father of psychoanalysis was one of the first to expose and address the problem of sexual abuse that was widespread in the Vienna of his time. In so doing he opened up a hornet's nest and found himself in hot water with his contemporaries, many of whom were themselves responsible for abuses. This caused him to compromise his views to accommodate the prevailing ethos. Instead of sexual abuse now being regarded as real with someone directly responsible, he took the view that it was still real for the victim but only as a subjective reality, in their own heads. The fact that he was unable to afford it an objective status became the unfortunate legacy of the psychiatric profession for generations. This view in turn found its way into the rest of society, influencing police, legal and medical professions alike. In effect it created one of the greatest blind spots in history where anyone who disclosed abuse would not be believed and even worse could be classed as insane. It has taken the psychiatric profession a long time to overcome that major hurdle and to state definitively that sexual abuse is an objective reality and does have long term and serious psychological consequences.

Thankfully we have now reached the stage where victims can be heard with love and compassion. Good procedures are in place for reporting and therapy models continue to improve. There are no excuses for sexual abuse. Understandably we still have a long way to go before we can recognise that the perpetrator also has a story and that there can be no full healing at societal level until we can adequately listen to both sides. Here it needs to be acknowledged that during the painful journey towards recovery, few if any victims are remotely interested in where their abuser is coming from and why they acted as they did. Indeed for anyone who has been abused or who is in recovery any attempt to look at the issue from both perspectives can be interpreted as minimising their pain and denying their hurt. Yet we also know that the answer is not to just lock up the abuser and throw away the key; a wider perspective is called for and a deeper understanding is needed.

The following story, where some iidentifying details have been changed, is offered in order to set abuse in a wider context and to look at it from both sides. It also may offer some insight as to why so many survivors remain stuck in anger and self-harm even after years of therapy work.

> *Michael, a man in his mid-thirties, was abused by a teacher for two years beginning when he was ten. This principal was highly regarded as an excellent teacher, very kind and considerate, and someone who always had his pupils' welfare at heart. He was also a pillar of the local community and involved in everything. Michael felt that he was the only one who knew this other side of him and would never be believed if he were to speak his truth. He also feared being ostracised by his local community who held this man in such high regard. So he kept silent. In his thirties, after a failed suicide attempt and the realisation that he was unable to maintain good relationships with women, he began to relate his problems back to his childhood abuse. He was quite intelligent so why had he performed so badly in secondary school and was always getting into trouble? Was there a reason as to why he thought himself to be bi-sexual; could it be related to his inappropriate sexual awakening by a male as he came into puberty? Was his tendency to drink too much and occasionally use drugs not his attempt to dull out the pain of carrying guilt and shame, feeling worthless and having such low self-esteem? He came to realise that the angry and troubled teenager he had become back then was far too removed from the happy-go-lucky child he had been and that the abuse had been the turning point.*

> *After many sessions of psychotherapy where he had told his story, cried his heart out, and revisited his painful shameful memories he began to feel stuck in his process. His therapist suggested that his problem at that stage was not just the hurt that had been done to him but the harm he was now doing to himself. The hurt belonged to the past and as such was not the full issue, but what was affecting him now was the harm he was inflicting on himself. In effect he came to see that he had become his own abuser. This meant that he didn't want to know the vulnerable child he had been back then. He still held that child responsible in some way for what had happened since he had visited the teacher's house on several occasions knowing what was going to happen.*

During the abuse a part of him had become split off and was still controlling his adult life. Now he came to understand that it was he who was keeping that part of himself out in the cold and he was faced with a choice: he could spend the rest of his life blaming his abuser for ruining his life and get nowhere or he could take responsibility for what he was still doing to himself and find healing. This insight was very challenging and became the major turning point where he was no longer stuck but able to continue his journey towards wholeness. It was his time of integration where he moved beyond victimhood and began to regain control of his life.

The teacher in question was charged with his offence along with a number of other charges relating to boys of the same age. He was convicted and spent time in jail. In psychotherapy his story began to unfold. It is included here not in any manner to take from the fact that he was both criminally and morally responsible for the terrible damage he caused, and that he deserved to be punished, but rather to shed some light of understanding on where he was coming from. His responsibility lay in the fact that he made seriously wrong choices that were very different from so many others who shared a similar background.

He was rejected from birth by his father and never received any affection or encouragement from him. As he grew older and began to assert his independence from about ten onwards the physical beatings grew so intense that he was brutalised and lived in terror of his father. He believed that there had to be something wrong with him to cause his father to be so violent. In effect a part of him had become split off and consigned to the depths of his unconscious and from there it became a controlling and compulsive force in his life.

At a conscious level this man, having been through such a dysfunctional childhood himself, resolved to be the good, kind and considerate father figure that so many of his pupils would be missing; and in this he largely succeeded. However, on many occasions during his career he admitted that a certain boy, always between ten and twelve would captivate his attention and he would be irresistibly drawn towards cultivating a 'special' relationship with that child. Initially he managed to maintain firm boundaries but slowly began to take risks and find ways of justifying his conscience. There came a point of no return where he realised that he was addicted to what he was doing and so under the guise of love was doing such terrible damage to his victims.

Without awareness he had no idea as to why he was attracted to boys of that particular age. It came as a major revelation to realise that it was his own ten- to twelve-year-old self that held such magical properties when projected onto an actual child. His abuse history had in fact been a shameful expression of his own misguided *search for wholeness. It was the beautiful child in himself, so terribly traumatised, that had been crying out for integration all along. He too had his story and a lot longer journey to go than any of his victims in order to live with his past and find the inner peace that comes with integration.*

HURT – HARM – HURT

With both victim and perpetrator a similar pattern was evident. In each case their story began with the hurt that was done to them. This translated into doing harm to themselves and them transferring hurt unto others. This model of, *hurt, harm* and *more hurt,* provides a useful way of understanding abuse in its many forms and why it happens. Not all offenders were sexually abused themselves; however, having been significantly traumatised at a particular age they went on to act out their trauma on someone else, often more or less of the same age. So the cycle was set to continue.

Such a model can also help to throw some light but *not* in any way to excuse the terrifying and criminal abuses that went on in religious- and state-run institutions. Hurt people perpetuate hurt just as soldiers being trained in torture techniques usually have to first undergo the same torture themselves in order to become desensitised. The kind of people who were responsible for such atrocities, in order to do such acts, had to have been seriously damaged individuals. In general, given the context of the time, they would have:

- Come from homes where discipline meant punishment and 'spare the rod and spoil the child' would have been the prevailing philosophy.

- Grown up in a society that was harsh and unforgiving; where children were not afforded respect and were to be seen but not heard. The care homes in many respects were reflections of the society at that time.

- Been through schools where education was shame based, corporal punishment was the norm and individuality was suppressed.

- Believed in a God of punishment who kept strict account of wrongdoing and demanded strict penances in order to purge the soul.

- Had a religious background that was heavily laden with guilt and fear and did nothing to promote the self-esteem of the individual.

- Experienced religious formation that broke their spirit, disregarded their emotions, denied their sexuality and brutalised their humanity.

- Been part of a religious system that believed in suffering as being good for the soul and apart from denial and repression didn't have a clue as to how to deal with issues of the past whether personal or ancestral.

All of the above were the unquestioned norms of society and religious life until very recent times. Only now can we see the hurt that was being inflicted and the inner harm that must have been going on for such horrendous abuses to have taken place. Particularly it was our brand of religion that, in the words of Patrick Kavanagh, was such 'an insult to the Incarnation' and a contradiction to the gospels, and that bears much responsibility for such a litany of abuses.

A SURVIVOR'S PERSPECTIVE

Those of us with an abuse background carry a legacy of negative messages that have been instilled into us from childhood and form much of the way we tend to see ourselves. These limit our ability to either think or feel positively and hold us back from moving forward into a broader life-giving way of living. Having constantly being given so many of these negative messages, both verbal and non-verbal, we take them to heart and believe them to be our truth. Victims of sexual abuse often mix up and confuse the difference between responsibility and blame; for most victims they are one and the same. If you are to blame then you have done something wrong, and if you have done something wrong then you are responsible for what has happened to you.

When we first hear someone suggesting that we take responsibility for the issues going on in our lives it feels as if all those who have hurt and abused us have been exonerated; everyone except ourselves. People say things like,' You're doing this to yourself, no one else is doing it to you,' or 'It's you that's wrong'. Most of us will automatically see this as a personal attack which just reinforces our negative belief system. It serves to confirm our worst fears and is not helpful.

Responsibility is different to blame, as it is not so much about what we did, but what we subconsciously took on as our belief system and continued that system or truth in negative ways towards ourselves. We continued to say and do to ourselves what was said and done to us. When we take responsibility seriously we are taking control. We are reclaiming our ability to respond which is exactly what responsibility means.

The blame game is exactly what robs us of the ability to be in control of our lives and keeps us victims rather than survivors. Blame makes us feel even worse about ourselves and hands over our personal power to people and circumstances. Even the spelling is significant, B-LAME. It is impossible to blame without being lame!

So responsibility is empowering while blame is disheartening and depressing.

=Responsibility looks forward, blame looks backward and most importantly responsibility recognises the fact that because of external factors success is not possible all of the time. Blame implies that if you had done, or had been, something different, the situation would have been different. The reality is that it is as it is and the challenge is how to deal with it best, give it meaning, and eventually to bring something good out of it.

Claire

FORGIVENESS – THE ROAD TO FREEDOM

The Crossroads of Forgiveness

The piece shown depicts forgiveness in terms of a crossroads. The past points downwards and carries the inner darkness of the wood. The present also is affected by that same darkness. The future points upwards and is clear. Forgiveness therefore is a moment in the present when we set ourselves free from the downward pull of the past and open out a bright new future. It is a divine gift which is not just for the person who has offended us, but also primarily for ourselves in order to set us free from the burden of resentment and bitterness.

Forgiveness is something everyone believes in until they are deeply hurt! There are two extremes to be avoided: one where we forgive too easily and too quickly and the other where we don't forgive at all. To forgive quickly and easily may seem like a Christian virtue but it doesn't take our wounded feelings into consideration. This may be just pseudo forgiveness and amounts to burying the hatchet while carefully marking the spot! We may be surprised that when the first opportunity arises our anger erupts and something derogatory just slips out of our mouths. Failure to forgive is resentment and can become our badge of identity forever holding us in the victim mode. The words we use in relation to grudges like 'holding', 'bearing' and 'nursing', are also the ones we use in relation to babies. As the baby gets bigger so do we get smaller.

In the summer of 2009 while engaged on sea-chaplaincy work the ship I was aboard made ports of call in different parts of the Baltic. One brief stopover was at Tallinn in Estonia. Tallinn had been part of the Communist Bloc and its residents would have lived for decades behind what was commonly called the 'Iron Curtain'. While there we had the opportunity to visit a communist museum which contained artefacts and information from that era. A woman in her early seventies gave a presentation which was really a description of her life under communist rule which had been her lot for so many years. It was truly a life that had been blighted.

Her story began when she was eight with her family being deported to Siberia. Her mother worked as a librarian and because of her education was deemed a threat to the Stalinist regime. Two weeks were spent travelling to Siberia on what amounted to a cattle train in freezing conditions. Her father had died the previous year so there were four children alone with their mother.

Conditions were deplorable when they arrived and starvation was rife. Her mother, however, managed to keep the family alive by gathering and selling sap from trees. All around them many other deportees starved to death. Three years later her mother was rearrested and brought to Moscow for trial. There she was sentenced to ten years' hard labour but given a choice: either to serve her sentence in Siberia or to remain in Moscow. Because her family were in Siberia she chose to return there but true to the communist determination to break the spirit she was forced to remain in Moscow. Back in Siberia the family still managed to survive with the eldest sister now in charge.

In her late teens Stalin died and the family were free to return and so made their way over a thousand miles back to Tallinn. In the aftermath of the war she became part of the Resistance Movement and was arrested by the Stasi who had an even worse reputation than Hitler's S.S. While in custody she was tortured and then spent years in a prison where the light was minimal and the sun never shone. The policy was that prisoners could never see the faces of their captors in case the regime collapsed and there would be reprisals. Eventually it did collapse and as a free woman her life resumed.

One of the visiting party then asked the question as to how she now felt in relation to the perpetuators and the collaborators who had taken the best years of her life. Her reply was quite astonishing; this is what she said:

> *Everybody in life is called to bear witness to the resilience of the human spirit. We all have to learn to be greater than whatever is done to us, what life throws at us, or even what we have done ourselves. The most important lesson of my life has been to practice the art of forgiveness. If I had not learned to forgive I would still be in prison and the one guarding me would not have a communist uniform but would be wearing my own clothes. Had I not forgiven I would still be in jail and be my own jailer. Communism is dead and gone, and thank God for that, but why should I allow them to have the last say over my life. It is by forgiveness that I have set myself free.*

THE PRACTICE OF FEAR OR FAITH

Believing is Seeing

What is faith? For so many it is an abstract concept. Many years of involvement with the sea and rescue services taught me that so many accidents and fatalities are caused by fear and panic while those who held their nerve so often survived against all the odds.

After being rescued many would say that it was their faith that sustained them. In Luke 8:22–25 when the disciples and Jesus are caught in the storm on the Sea of Galilee they wake up Jesus in fright to tell him that they are lost. He rebukes the wind and the sea and it grows calm. He then asks them the question, *Where was their faith?* The implication was that they did have faith but were exercising it in the wrong manner: that there was more in the power of the wind and the sea to overwhelm them than in his power to sustain them.

A useful acronym for understanding FAITH is – *Fantastic Adventure In Trusting Him.*

In Hebrews (Heb.11:1) faith is described as 'the assurance of things hoped for and the conviction of things not seen.' It is so much more than simple assent to a set of beliefs that worshippers recite every week in the Creed. Something of the essence of faith is contained in the above acronym, an adventure in trust. According to St Augustine, 'faith is believing what you don't see and the reward of faith is seeing what you have believed.' Here he introduces the notion of believing as seeing, so our understanding of faith could be extended to seeing the invisible so we can do the impossible. Every created thing begins with a thought and then from that thought the vision is formed. From someone believing in the vision and putting the required energy into it, the original thought becomes a reality. The initial step in faith is usually the most difficult since it entails 'walking on water' and having the courage to be fearless about appearing foolish. From this broader understanding of faith it becomes clear that whether one be a believer or an atheist we exercise either faith or fear – which is its opposite – every day of our lives.

A useful acronym for understanding FEAR is – *Fantasy Experienced As Real.*

Fear has its roots in yesterday, makes today feel safe and is our enemy of tomorrow. It alerts us to the perils of 'now' because of what happened before. It appears to keep us safe but is in fact our only obstacle to joy. An example of this is where someone has experienced hurt because of a broken relationship. When opportunities arise to get to know someone new they are not availed of out of fear of being hurt again. The fear belongs to the past, it protects the comfort zone of the present and in so doing robs the future of possibilities.

- Faith expands our world, fear constricts it.
- Faith sees a positive outcome, fear sees the worst scenario.
- Faith places us above our circumstances, fear puts us below.
- Faith risks the game of life, fear plays it safe.
- Faith extends the comfort zone, fear reduces it.
- Faith makes mistakes, fear makes excuses.

- Faith allows us to walk on water, fear makes us sink.
- Faith sees divine order, fear sees chaos.
- Faith conquers, fear falters.
- Faith creates that which is believed, fear does likewise.

Faith is like using a muscle; it requires exercise before it can take on a big strain. So don't be afraid to start small. For a bit of faith training, try the following:

When driving into town and traffic is heavy say, 'Lord, I need a parking space in such and such a place'. That's the *prayer*. Next comes the *believing*. If we look at the volume of cars and start thinking, 'This is a very unrealistic prayer and I am going to be going round in circles for ages,' then we will not be disappointed – we will get what we expect. On the other hand, if we keep visualising in our minds the exact parking space that we need, almost without fail it will appear or else we won't have to wait for very long to find someone pulling out of a parking space in front of us.

> *A businessman drove into a city where the traffic was chaotic so he got delayed. He was due to speak at a conference and he arrived with minutes to spare but the car park was jammed. He prayed, 'Lord, if you get me a space I'll give up drink, give up smoking and stop womanising.' Just then a car pulled out ahead of him. 'It's okay, Lord,' he said, 'you can cancel that request; I've just found a space!'*

When we are ill we go to a doctor whose name we can't pronounce. He or she gives us a prescription we can't read and we go to a pharmacist we don't know, who gives us medication we don't understand and that we believe is going to make us better. That is faith! Living a life of faith also involves transforming the apparent negatives into positives. With the eyes of faith we see:

- That stumbling blocks can become stepping stones.
- That setbacks can become springboards.
- That mountains can become molehills.
- That problems can become opportunities.
- That mistakes can become learning experiences.
- That disappointments can become Divine appointments.
- That caterpillars can become butterflies.
- That ends can become new beginnings.
- That sad departures can be joyful homecomings.
- That history will eventually be seen as his Story.

Whatsoever you ask for in faith believe that you <u>have already</u>
received and it will be granted. (Matt. 21:22)

From this Divine promise we can say that faith is living in the reality of what is not yet, but as if it were an accomplished fact. At the same time being aware that how and when the answer comes may not be in the time frame or manner in which I think it should.

There is an intrinsic connection between the exercise of faith and having a positive optimistic outlook on life. The *Optimist Creed* was authored in 1912 by Christian D. Larson and it was adopted as Optimist International's creed in 1922 and has inspired thousands ever since.

THE OPTIMIST CREED

To be so strong that nothing can disturb your peace of mind.

To talk health, happiness, and prosperity to every person you meet.

To make all your friends feel that there is something worthwhile in them.

To look at the sunny side of everything … even when things are going wrong.

To think only of the best, to work only for the best, and to expect only the best.

To be just as enthusiastic about the success of others as you are about your own.

To forget the mistakes of the past and press on to greater things that lie ahead.

To wear a cheerful expression at all times and give a smile to every one you meet.

To give so much time to improving yourself that you have no time to criticise others.

To be too large for worry, too noble for anger and too strong for fear.

To think well of yourself and to proclaim this fact to the
world, not in loud words, but in great deeds.

To live in the faith that the whole world is on your side, so
long as you are true to the best that is in you.

A CHECKLIST FOR SPIRITUAL GROWTH

- An increasing ability to live in the present and enjoy each moment.

- Lightness of spirit where I don't take myself too seriously.

- Having more compassion towards myself and others.

- Acting spontaneously rather than on fears based on past experiences.

- Having a sense of purpose and destiny.

- A willingness to act with courage and extend my comfort zone.

- A loss of interest in judging other people.

- No longer being shocked by the actions of others.

- Taking things with gratitude rather than for granted.

- A loss of interest in conflict or violence of any form.

- A decreasing tendency to worry and increased sense of providence.

- Frequent episodes of overwhelming deep appreciation.

- Contented feelings of connectedness with others and nature.

- Frequent attacks of smiling, often for no apparent reason.

- An increased tendency to go with the flow and let things happen.

- A greater capacity for looking and seeing the bigger picture.

- Less struggle and trying to make things happen.

- Feeling more susceptible to the love of others.

- An uncontrollable urge to extend love to all creatures

A Spirituality of Healing and Integration

A SUMMARY OF CONTENTS

as

B-ATTITUDES FOR TODAY

Blessed are those who live life with open hands,
for they are ready to receive.

Blessed are those whose love grants freedom,
for they shall be greatly loved.

Blessed are those who have journeyed within,
for they shall not go without.

Blessed are those who give what they cannot keep,
for they shall gain what they cannot lose.

Blessed are those who draw from their inner well,
for the blessings of life are theirs.

Blessed are those who live with non-attachment,
for their spirits can soar like the eagle.

Blessed are those who own their shadow,
for they have discovered the secret of wholeness.

Blessed are those who have befriended their anger,
for they have released their creativity.

Blessed are those who believe what they cannot see,
for they shall see that which they have believed.

Blessed are those who have learned to forgive,
for they have unlocked the gates of their own prison.

Blessed are those who have released their departed,
for they shall live in perpetual communion.

LISTENING FOR THE WORD

When we listen something new is born!

The entire Bible is the story of God's gradual revelation of himself culminating in the sending of his Son who is his definitive word. Jesus is the image of the invisible God who in his humanity is our most accurate reflection of the Divine. One teaching that is consistent throughout the scriptures is that God does speak to his people, that his word is powerful and does not return without having accomplished that which it was sent to do. (Isa. 55:11) In the First Book of Samuel, Chapter 2 there is the lovely story of how the young prophet began to listen to the voice of the Lord. Although the event happened nearly three thousand years ago the perception was that like our own times it was rare for the Lord to speak in those days and visions were uncommon. However, we are also told that the Lamp of God had not gone out; there was some flicker of faith still evident.

From his birth Samuel had been consecrated to the Lord by his mother, Hannah, who being childless had, in great distress, prayed for a child and was granted her request. While spending time in the temple at Shiloh he hears a voice calling, 'Samuel, Samuel'. Thinking that it is the old priest, Eli, who is calling he goes to him to be told that he is not being called and to go back to sleep. Only when this happens a third time does Eli realise that it is the Lord who is calling the boy and his advice is that the next time he hears that voice to say, 'Speak Lord, your servant is listening.' Once again the voice calls and this time Samuel is ready to hear and as he grows up we are told that he is careful 'not to let any word of the Lord fall to the ground.'

To hear God's word in our lives depends not so much on our ability to hear but on trust in and openness to God's ability to speak and get through to us in spite of our deafness. While he can speak to us in an infinite variety of ways we sometimes experience whispers of Spirit that can be like a still, small voice. What sets them apart from other voices in our heads is that these carry a compelling authority and a sense of peace. In fact it is when we have cultivated the art of silence through meditation and prayer that we are most likely to clearly distinguish the voice of Spirit. It could be compared to tuning in to a particular wavelength on radio except that it is the 'silent' channel.

Occasionally such whispers take us completely by surprise and point us in a direction that at the time doesn't make a lot of sense. Around the turn of the millennium, while engaged in preaching a sermon, I was surprised to hear the words, 'Go to the wood'. Initially this seemed strange as there were no woods in the area and if it meant to take up woodwork I had no background or training of any sort. The word did not go away and so I began an amazing adventure with wood. Looking back it was like the small mustard seed that Jesus spoke of in Matt. 13:31–32, where he said that although it was tiny it had the potential to become a tree so large that the birds of the air could find shelter in its branches. Quite literally over the course of a few short years this is in fact what has happened.

An initial sale of pieces on exhibition raised nearly five thousand euros for children orphaned through AIDS in Uganda. Local fundraising continued for this charity and over a number of years raised close to one hundred thousand euros. As new skills with the work developed it became possible to make more and more symbols for use in preaching and teaching. These have been used to good effect in hundreds of seminars and retreats throughout Ireland and elsewhere and have added an entire new dimension to each presentation.

From the initial series of seminars came the suggestion of committing the content to print and so the first book in the *Wood You Believe* series came to fruition. I did not believe the art of writing to be my forte and I knew nothing of the world of book production or publishing. Still, that initial whisper of Spirit had a sustaining and providential element whereby the right people and stories came my way exactly when I needed them. This has been the case with all six volumes and the experience of writing them and making the accompanying symbols has always been a source of great joy and never a burden.

Today the proceeds from books go mostly towards those who are homeless and destitute, so as the adventure with wood continues to expand it is now like a large tree and literally does provide shelter for those who are most in need.

From a tiny whisper containing just four words, 'Go to the wood', has evolved an entire ministry that now touches thousands of lives and being a part of it continues to be one of the most exciting adventures of my life.

It is by its fruit that we ultimately can test whether a word is from God or not. This little book is just one such fruit that hopefully provides a good measure of spiritual nourishment.

COVER PIECE BACKGROUND STORY

A rather lovely and true story is associated with the cover piece depicted on this book. A couple lived on the outskirts of a village. They were non-churchgoers with limited connection to the wider community. He was from a Catholic background while she had been baptised Church of England. The husband took seriously ill and knew that he was dying. He was greatly concerned for his wife who was going to be left on her own and isolated.

Weeks later, he passed on and at his funeral mass people were coming forward to receive Communion. It seemed as if the only one not coming was his wife and a wave of sorrow passed over the priest in relation to her. If anyone desperately needed the reassurance of Communion just then it had to be her, even if it were her first time in church. To his surprise he heard a whisper of Spirit saying, 'Bring her Communion, I want her to be in communion.' To do so would have meant breaking the rules and putting the cart before the horse – there had been neither instruction given nor any interest shown. Still, in response to that whisper he went down the church and asked, 'Would you like to receive Holy Communion?' She smiled and said, 'Yes'.

Nearly a year later, the lady appeared to be doing very well; she had continued to attend church regularly and had begun to integrate herself into the community. One day she asked the priest if he had noticed the difference in her and how she had become so involved. 'Of course,' he replied, 'it's so obvious and wonderful to see.' 'Do you know when it began?' she asked and he replied, 'No.' 'The day of my husband's funeral when you came and asked me if I wanted to receive Communion. You didn't know this but all my life I have prayed and my constant prayer was that I would belong. Just at that moment, in my hour of greatest need, I knew that my prayer was being answered and I also knew where I wanted to belong.'

She then went through a period of instruction and months later had a huge community celebration where she committed her life to Christ. It was during that beautiful ceremony that the cover-piece sculpture was presented to her to mark her journey and honour the occasion.

ABOUT THE AUTHOR

Fr Jim Cogley was born in Wexford in 1954. He trained for the priesthood in St Patrick's College Maynooth, where he took degrees in English, Philosophy and Theology. Ordained in 1980 for the Diocese of Ferns in Ireland, he has a deep love of the sea which is reflected in his involvement with the work of Sea Chaplaincy. Formerly based in Kilmore Quay for most of his pastoral life and now in Oylegate, he has many years teaching experience and is a counselling supervisor. As a psychotherapist, he trained in the Jungian tradition. His particular area of interest is that of Intergenerational Healing and how the past that is unacknowledged can still influence the present.

His innovative, self-taught woodworking skills, developed in recent years, provide a unique opportunity to present the age-old truths of life and spirituality in the form of symbols that speak to the soul. Many of the seminars he conducts throughout the country on topics such as those covered in the 'Wood you Believe' series involve the use of such symbols. His concept of a Memorial Trail and Garden to people lost at sea, located in Kilmore Quay, and the recently opened Raphael's Healing Garden along with The Tree of Life in Oylegate are now major visitor attractions.

The latest publication Vol 6 - The Spiritual Self, has received very positive reviews in national papers and magazines and been described as one of the most important contributions to religious journalism in recent times.

A SPIRITUALITY OF HEALING AND INTEGRATION

A Spirituality of Healing and Integration, offers much needed wisdom for the spiritual landscape we find ourselves in at this time. The inspiring symbolism, intertwined with scripture, story and insights from psychology makes it a compelling read. It outlines succinctly and clearly where we have come from and where we find ourselves as church in Ireland today. But it doesn't stop there, it navigates us towards a spirituality of the future and offers a direction in which we can be orientating ourselves in religious practice.

****

'Life is like a voyage on the sea of history, often dark and stormy, a voyage in which we watch for the stars that indicate the route.' (Spe Salvi 49)

In Vol 6 of Wood You Believe, through scripture and sculpture, story and self-acceptance, Jim Cogley encourages his readers to face the turbulence of today's faith voyage and drop anchor in the Spirit of God within.

Shadow and light, wholeness and imperfection are embraced on the self-abandon voyage leading towards the 'living water welling up within to eternal life'. (John 4:14)

Phrases such as, 'The Samaritan woman went away with the well'; 'When we listen something new is born'; 'Transformation'; 'Under new management'; 'Let go, let God'; are like pop-ups that sparkle anew throughout A Spirituality of Healing and Integration leading the reader to 'Jesus, the true light, the sun that has risen above the shadow of history.' (Spe Salvi 49)

Bishop Eamonn Walsh

ISBN 978-0-9557110-6-0

www.ingramcontent.com/pod-product-compliance
Lightning Source LLC
Chambersburg PA
CBHW041217030426
42336CB00023B/3375